Colorado

COLORADO BY ROAD

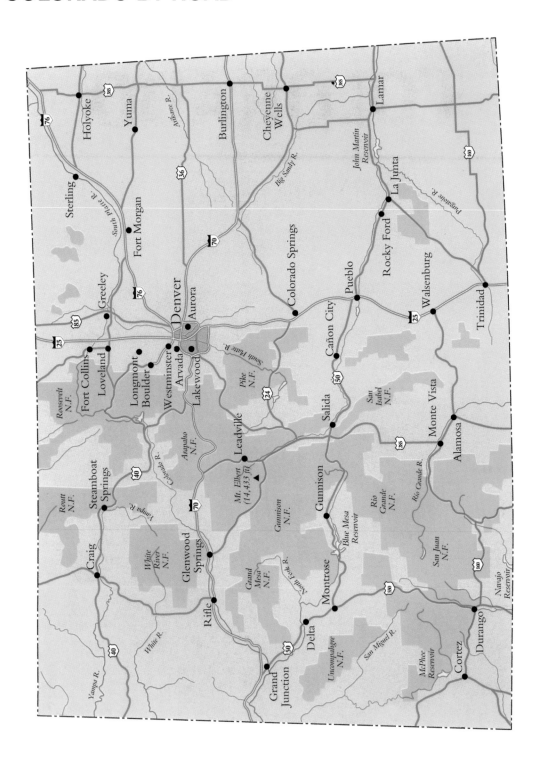

Celebrate the States

Colorado

Eleanor Ayer and Dan Elish

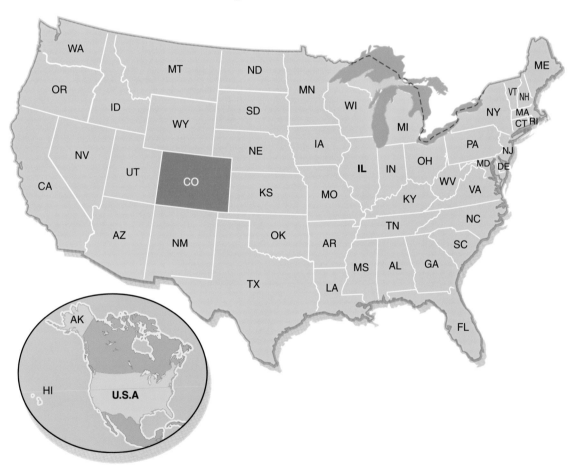

mc Marshall Cavendish
Benchmark
New York

Marshall Cavendish Benchmark
99 White Plains Road
Tarrytown, NY 10591-9001
www.marshallcavendish.us

Library of Congress Cataloging-in-Publication Data

Elish, Dan.
Colorado / by Dan Elish and Eleanor Ayer—2nd ed.
p. cm. — (Celebrate the states)
Summary: Provides comprehensive information on the geography, history, governmental structure,
economy, cultural diversity, and landmarks of Colorado—Provided by publisher.
Includes bibliographical references and index.
ISBN0-7614-2019-3
1. Colorado—Juvenile literature. I. Ayer, Eleanor H. II. Title III. Series.
F776.3.E45 2006
978.8—dc22   2005015944

Editor: Christine Florie
Editorial Director: Michelle Bisson
Art Director: Anahid Hamparian
Series Designer: Adam Mietlowski

Photo research by Candlepants Incorporated

Cover Photo: Terry W. Eggers/Corbis
The photographs in this book are used by permission and through the courtesy of; *Corbis*: Scott T.
Smith, 8; W. Perry Conway, 11, 19, 85, 114; David Muench, 12, 98, 102, 119, 135; Joseph
Sohm/ChromoSohm Inc., 14; 15, 33, 91, 125; Marc Muench, 20; Tom Brakefield, 22; George H.H.
Huey, 24; Buddy Mays, 28; Ken Reading, 42, 87; Gabe Palmer, 50; James L. Amos, 55; Jim
Richardson, 57, 83; Dean Congers, 60; Reuters, 62, 67, 72, 129; Ted Spiegel, 74; Grafton Marshall
Smith, 77; Craig Aurness, 78; Tom Bean, 82; Bill Ross, 92; Richard T. Nowitz, 97; Vince Streano,
103; Lester Lefkowitz, 108; Kennan Ward, 111; Buddy Mays, 113; Rick Wilking/Reuters, 121;
Sygma/Visser Robert, 127; Wally McNamee, 132; Michael S. Lewis, 138; Annie Griffiths Belt, back
cover. *Art Wolfe/Photo Researchers Inc.*: 23. *Western History Collection/Denver Public Library*: 27, 29.
Colorado State Historical Society: 35, 38, 41. *The Image Works*: Sean Cayton, 48; Joe Sohm, 95.
Index Stock: E. J. West, 81; Ron Ruhoff, 105; Patricia Barry Levy, 123.

Printed in China

3 5 6 4

Contents

Colorado Is . . .

Colorado is breathtakingly beautiful . . .

O beautiful for spacious skies,
For amber waves of grain,
For purple mountain majesties
Above the fruited plain! . . .

—from *America the Beautiful*, by Katharine Lee Bates,
inspired by the view from Pikes Peak

"[Colorado's] scenery bankrupts the English language."
—Theodore Roosevelt, twenty-sixth president of the United States

"Sometimes it seems like the mountains have mountains here. And the
sky just goes on and on."

—Mike Conniff, journalist

Its beauty has drawn people for centuries . . .

"It was something, at last to stand upon the storm-rent crown of this
lonely sentinel of the Rocky Range, on one of the mightiest of the
vertebrae of the backbone of the North American continent, and to see
the waters start for both oceans."
—Isabella Bird, Englishwoman who climbed Longs Peak in 1873

"Being Molly for even the six months it took to make the film meant so
much to me that I bought a small piece of her Colorado, close to
Leadville. . . . I go there as often as possible to enjoy the wonder, beauty
and serenity of [the] mountains and give myself a spiritual treat."
—Debbie Reynolds, played Molly Brown in
The Unsinkable Molly Brown

Those who live here tend to stay.

"I will never leave my Shining Mountains."

—Ute Chief Ouray, to U.S. government agents

"You move to California because you want heat, you move to Alaska because you want cold, and you move to Mars because you're a nonbreathing mutant. But you don't have to move from Colorado, because you got it all right here, baby!"

—T. C. Ritz, sixth-grade Colorado student

Still, the people of Colorado know that there are challenges ahead.

"We meet at a time of challenge, not of crisis. We meet at a time when we are called to work together."

—Governor Bill Owens, addressing the Colorado state legislature in 2003

"Colorado has problems just like any state. In the last couple of years we've had unemployment, a drought and forest fires! But we always manage to work things out. Besides, we have all those beautiful mountains. They get us through the tough times."

—Harvey Wexler, first-grade teacher

Besides the state's awesome beauty, the sun shines here three hundred days a year. The outlook of most people is as bright as the Colorado sun. With its golden fields of wheat and corn, its majestic Rocky Mountains, and the opportunity for a year-round outdoor life, it's no wonder that newcomers arrive in droves. Some old-timers are saddened by the recent waves of immigrants. They complain about overcrowded highways, huge housing developments, and the "Californication of Colorado." But who can blame people for heeding the words of the singer John Denver: "Guess he'd rather be in Colorado"?

Chapter One

Mile-High State

When the western songwriter Utah Phillips sang of going "Out West where the states are square," Colorado was one of the states he had in mind. Actually, Colorado (meaning "color red" in Spanish) is more of a rectangle—276 miles north to south and 387 miles east to west.

Some folks say that if you took a giant flatiron to Colorado and pressed down the mountains, you'd have a state as large as Texas. There are fifty-four mountain peaks in Colorado that reach 14,000 feet high. There are a thousand more mountains that rise to 10,000 feet. In fact, the state has so many mountains that some of them haven't even been named! Colorado is the eighth-largest state, and all those mountains easily make it the highest.

Stretching north to south through the center of the state and into the Southwest are Colorado's tallest mountains. They are part of the Rocky Mountains, which run from Canada down into Mexico. Colorado has twenty-eight major ranges. The Front Range, on the eastern side of the Rockies, is the biggest and best known.

Rocky Mountain National Park contains seventy-eight mountain peaks that are more than 12,000 feet high. Longs Peak is the highest in the park at 14,255 feet (opposite).

Yet the state is by no means all mountains. Mountains are only one of its three major landforms. In the east are the plains—huge, flat, treeless expanses of grass. In the central and southwestern parts of the state are the mountains. Western Colorado is covered by a vast plateau that stretches above the surrounding land.

FRUITED PLAINS AND ROLLING FOOTHILLS

Colorado's High Plains are part of the Great Plains, which spread across the midwestern section of North America. The plains are the top of thousands of feet of dirt washed down as the outer edges of the Rocky Mountains eroded. In some places the bed of dirt and rock is almost four miles thick. As the plains slope eastward, farther away from the mountains, the dirt and rock bed becomes thinner. Near the Kansas border the base is only about a mile thick.

The Colorado plains are home to few people and animals, and even fewer trees. When the explorer Stephen Harriman Long went west in 1820, he called this area "the Great American Desert." The plains, he said, were "almost wholly unfit for cultivation." How wrong he was! Today, thanks to irrigation and improved farming methods, eastern Colorado is one of the most productive agricultural regions in the country.

The Front Range runs along the eastern foothills of the Rockies. Eighty percent of Colorado's people live in the strip from Fort Collins south through the Denver/Boulder area to Colorado Springs and Pueblo. The 2.5 million people who have since settled along this corridor have created an urban sprawl. The Front Range is now largely housing developments with little open space in between.

For the first time in thirty years, Denver's air quality is meeting federal regulations. There still are problems, however. Heavy car traffic leads

The Eastern Plains of Colorado are a section of the broader Great Plains. Precipitation is low there; however, winter wheat thrives in this region.

to high carbon monoxide levels. The mountains trap this polluted air, creating Denver's ugly "brown cloud." Fortunately, the city is investing millions of dollars in a light-rail transportation system, which should help with the problem.

THE MOUNTAIN REGION

Colorado's mountains are the source of many of the country's large rivers. Running along the tops of the mountains north to south is an imaginary line called the Continental Divide. Rivers that rise (begin) east of the divide—including the Platte, Arkansas, Rio Grande, and Big Thompson—eventually flow into the Gulf of Mexico. Rivers that rise on

The Yampa River rises in northwestern Colorado. It is a tributary of the Green River.

its western side flow into the Pacific. Among these are the Colorado, Gunnison, Green, Yampa, and Dolores.

The San Juan Mountains in southwestern Colorado get nearly eighty inches of precipitation a year, mostly in the form of snow. Each year during spring in the San Juans and elsewhere, rivers fill with water as the snow melts. But sometimes the snow doesn't melt. If it is too cold, it accumulates year after year and eventually turns into ice. When this huge pile of ice is heavy enough to move slowly downhill, a glacier is born.

The state has several glaciers and many large rivers but few natural lakes. Those that are natural are usually small and found in the high mountains. Most large lakes are reservoirs for water storage, and many of them are man-made.

At high altitudes the weather can be unpredictable. Even experienced mountaineers can be caught off guard by rapid changes in the weather. In the mountains, warns Janet Robertson, the author of *Day Hikes on the Colorado Trail*, "Snow storms, gale force winds, stifling heat, [freezing] rains . . . can [happen] on any given summer day." Winter weather can be even more severe.

High-altitude plants and animals must be tough to endure harsh weather, to survive in thin air, and to withstand the burning rays of the sun. But they are fragile, too. When hiking boots trample spongy tundra grasses, it can take years for the vegetation to recover, if it ever does. Pollution from cities is also very harmful to mountain plant and animal life.

Nestled among the mountain ranges of central Colorado, near the Continental Divide, are four huge natural parks. These large, flat valleys were once covered with soft, green grasses and dotted with herds of bison and antelope. Today farmers raise hay and other crops in the parks, and ranchers graze large herds of cattle.

The northernmost of these parks is North Park, once a favorite hunting ground of the Ute Indians. Just to the south and west of the Continental Divide lies Middle Park, where the Colorado River rises. It gets very cold in Middle Park in the winter. The town of Fraser often appears in the news as the "coldest spot in the nation."

In South Park, which is west of Denver near Fairplay, are the headwaters of the South Platte River. In 1859 prospectors rushed there

Cattle graze in a pasture beneath the Sneffels Mountain Range.

searching for gold. The fourth and southernmost of the parks, the San Luis Park, is so arid that it is almost a desert. For nearly 150 years this valley has been home to many Hispanics.

BUFFALO BILL: THE STORY BEHIND THE LEGEND

William F. Cody (1846–1917), a former Pony Express rider, earned the nickname "Buffalo Bill" when he was hired in 1867 to supply meat for the men building the Kansas Pacific Railroad through eastern Colorado. With 60 million American bison roaming the Great Plains, buffalo (as we often call them) were a plentiful target. During one seventeen-month period Cody killed more than four thousand buffalo.

By the early 1870s the buffalo slaughter reached one million animals a year. By 1895 this great American beast was nearly extinct, and the government stepped in to stop the slaughter. Today some Colorado ranchers raise buffalo, but no longer do millions of those grand creatures roam free with the deer and the antelope.

When buffalo hunting came to an end, Bill Cody organized his Wild West Show. The entertainment included wild beasts, bands of Indians, cowboys, and cowgirls—among them the famous markswoman Annie Oakley. Buffalo Bill's popular Wild West show toured the United States and Europe.

When Buffalo Bill died in 1917, he was buried on Lookout Mountain near Golden. His grave was covered with tons of concrete to make certain that the rival town of Cody, Wyoming would not steal his remains for burial there.

LAND AND WATER

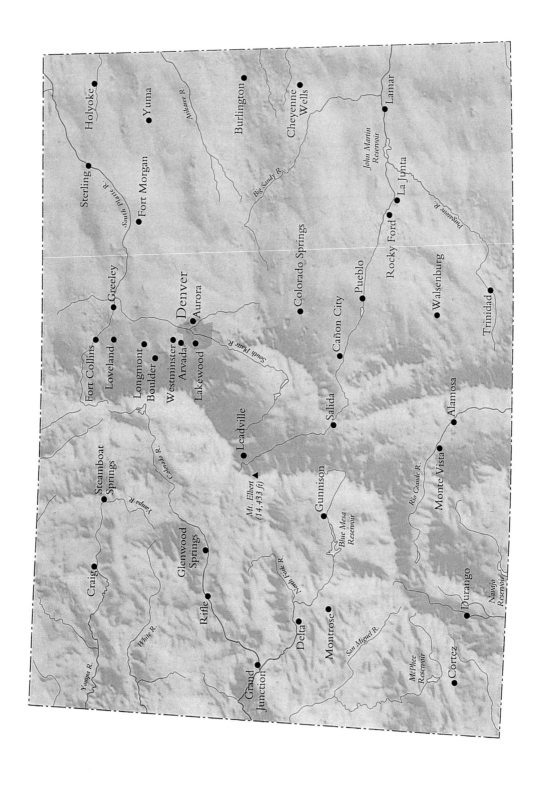

THE WESTERN SLOPE

The Colorado Plateau covers parts of four western states: Colorado, Utah, Arizona, and New Mexico. In fact, at the Four Corners Monument in southwestern Colorado, you can put one hand in Utah and one in Colorado, one foot in Arizona and the other in New Mexico. It's the only point in the United States where you can be in four states at once!

It took millions of years for nature to build the Colorado Plateau. When the Rocky Mountains were pushed up from inside the earth, the plateau rose up with them. Unlike the plains, where the rock slopes down from the mountains, the plateau remained flat. Even so, this region is called the Western Slope.

Western Colorado is less densely populated than the Front Range, and the lifestyle is generally more laid-back. The region's two largest cities, Grand Junction in the center and Durango in the southwest, are small compared with Front Range cities. The climate on the plateau is much drier than in the rest of the state, but fruit orchards thrive there. Peach grower Earl Brown explains his success: "The Palisade Cliffs and the Grand Mesa Towers and the mountains to the east all hold the daytime heat and keep the temperature at night warm enough for the trees to grow. That warm draft is even called the peach wind." But the mild climate that makes fruit grow so well has also attracted many new people. The Western Slope is now dealing with a population boom.

The Colorado Plateau is rich in minerals. Oil, one of the most important, is found in shale, a rock that splits easily into thin layers. Oil shale is a valuable source of fuel. Uranium is another type of fuel found buried in the plateau. Nuclear power is produced by splitting its atoms. Vanadium, often found near uranium, is an element used to harden steel. And where there is oil, deposits of coal and natural gas are often found, too.

It's no mystery why the plateau is so rich in fuels. The Western Slope once was home to massive dinosaurs. One hundred and fifty million years ago the area had a warm, wet climate, with trees like those you might find in a humid jungle today. Fossils—bones and imprints from prehistoric times—have left clues as to what life was like in Colorado long ago. Coal, oil, and natural gas are called fossil fuels because they were created from decaying plant and animal remains during the dinosaur era.

North of Grand Junction is Dinosaur National Monument, once populated by such huge herbivores as apatosaurus (brontosaurus), diplodocus, and stegosaurus and their meat-eating enemy, allosaurus. At Dinosaur Quarry scientists are continually uncovering new fossils in the park. One wall there, which is enclosed for viewing, displays some 1,600 dinosaur bones.

WEIRD WEATHER

Because it is far from any large body of water, Colorado tends to be quite dry. On many summer afternoons, however, people can expect a thunderstorm, often with tornado warnings, on the eastern plains and along the Front Range. During the winter a "stockman's advisory" warns ranchers of danger to livestock from blizzards.

Colorado's climate is moderate; that is, temperatures are neither extremely hot nor extremely cold, but they can be very surprising. Snow has fallen in August, and the thermometer can reach 72 degrees Fahrenheit in January. The chinook is a warm dry wind, which locals call a snow eater. In winter the cold, wet air west of the mountains is pushed up and over the peaks. Near the top the air drops its moisture in the form of snow, which warms the air. Then a warm wind, the chinook, rushes down the eastern slope at great speeds—more than 100 miles per hour at times—melting the snow below.

Weather conditions can change quickly in the mountains. Summer storms keep this valley green.

Weather stations in Colorado often report "upslope conditions" when air moves up the sides of the mountains instead of down. The mix of air masses during upslope conditions can bring heavy precipitation. "Hail Alley," which runs roughly along the Front Range, receives more hail than anywhere else in the United States.

A thick mist called Cheyenne fog is another unusual bit of Colorado weather. This mist often gathers around high mountain peaks. Pikes Peak

Fog clings to peaks at the Colorado National Monument.

has Cheyenne fog about every third day, yet below in Colorado Springs there is fog only about twelve days a year.

With its weird weather, desolate plains, and awesome mountains, the settlement of Colorado was left to the strong-hearted. On his first visit west, in 1870, Horace Greeley, the founder and editor of the *New York Tribune*, proclaimed, "We seem to have reached the acme of barrenness and desolation." But like many newcomers, Greeley eventually fell in love with the state. He returned with a group of pioneers to found the Union Colony, where the city of Greeley now stands. Back home, he famously urged his readers, "Go West, young man, go West."

ENDANGERED IN COLORADO

"When the grizzly is gone," wrote John McGuire of *Outdoor Life* magazine, "we shall have lost the [noblest] specimen of wildlife [in] the western wilderness." Today the Colorado grizzly is gone. Like other endangered animals, the grizzly found it impossible to coexist with the growing numbers of human beings. Other animals, such as the gray wolf, the lynx, and the wolverine, have nearly disappeared.

Fish are also victims of Colorado's growth. Squawfish, known to reach six feet and weigh eighty pounds, have become endangered by the damming of the Colorado River. This, along with pollution caused by industrial and human waste, drastically slashed the numbers of humpback chub, razorback sucker, and green cutthroat trout.

Many great birds that once lived in Colorado became endangered during the twentieth century, their habitats severely reduced or destroyed by people. The peregrine falcon, mascot of the United States Air Force Academy, is endangered but is making a comeback, as are the whooping crane and America's national bird, the bald eagle.

Twenty years ago bald eagles were hard to come by in Colorado. However, now on the endangered species list, their numbers have increased to about eight hundred.

ANIMALS ON THE COMEBACK

Despite the loss of natural habitats, Colorado is doing what it can to protect the state's animals. Nesting pairs of sandhill cranes, piping plovers, and prairie chickens have been reintroduced to the Centennial State and are starting to breed again. Great pains are being taken to protect the Gunnison sage grouse, a nesting bird that is found only in western Colorado and eastern Utah. With barely three thousand left in the world, wildlife organizations have been working with cattle ranchers to limit grazing on the sagebrush that the grouse need to live.

"We've had to get the cattle to graze at certain times and in limited amounts," states a worker with the Colorado Nature Conservancy. "Luckily, the ranchers have been very cooperative. After all, protecting the grouse also helps them protect their land and way of life."

The Gunnison sage grouse has elaborate mating rituals. Pairs return to the exact same courtship spot, or lek, each spring. It is the task of the Colorado Division of Wildlife to make sure that these leks remain undeveloped. As one ranger put it, "If a lek turned into a housing subdivision, it would ruin everything."

In 1999 the Canada lynx, a cousin of the bobcat, was reintroduced into the western part of the state. The first year or two were difficult. As the lynx struggled to find appropriate dens, about half the animals perished. But in the summer of 2003, the lynx managed to make six dens. More important, sixteen kittens were born. Clearly, the lynx are breeding. The hope of the Colorado Division of Wildlife is that some of these newborns will survive their first year and give birth to kittens of their own.

"Now that we have kittens, we need to see the lynx population grow," noted Toby White, a ranger. "Then we'll know that the program has really worked."

Recognizing the dwindling numbers of Canada lynx, Colorado placed the species on its endangered species list in 1976. Today about 170 lynx have been released into the San Juan Mountains.

Chapter Two

From Pueblos to Condos

Some of the state's first inhabitants roamed the Colorado Plateau, hunting animals and gathering nuts and berries. By about AD 1 these people were weaving baskets to hold their food, so historians call them Basket Makers. These were the first of the ancient Puebloans, or Anasazi.

Though the ancient Puebloans were hunters and gatherers, they also farmed, growing corn, beans, and squash. Some archaeologists believe that they were able to grow up to forty bushels of corn per acre, enough food to provide for a population that may have reached nearly 20,000 people. Many ancient Puebloans cultivated their own small gardens, which had the added benefit of attracting rabbits and birds for hunting. The people also hunted elk, deer, bighorn sheep, and antelope.

By AD 750 the ancient Puebloans were building their homes from adobe (bricks made from sun-dried mud and straw). Communities exchanged goods through an elaborate trade network. In later years they built their houses tucked under huge overhanging sandstone cliffs, which you can see today in Mesa Verde National Park or Hovenweep National Monument.

Located in Mesa Verde National Park, Cliff Palace is the largest cliff dwelling in North America. It is the remains of an Anasazi, or ancient Puebloan, settlement.

Most historians believe that droughts in the summer and frosts in the winter eventually forced the ancient Puebloans to move in search of land with a better climate and more reliable water sources. By AD 1300 the ancient Puebloans had abandoned the Four Corners region, heading south to mix with other cultures. This mix became known as the Pueblo Indians.

FOR GOLD, GOD, AND GLORY

In the 1500s Spanish conquistadores (conquerors) arrived from Mexico. For more than two hundred years the Spanish poured in— adventurers in search of gold and missionaries spreading the teachings of Christ. In 1706 the explorer Juan de Ulibarri camped with a party of men near present-day Pueblo. Raising his sword high, Ulibarri proclaimed, "In the name of our king, Don Philip V, we claim this land for Spain. Long live the king!"

Contact with the Spanish was devastating to the Pueblo tribes. For example, the Spanish introduced deadly smallpox, causing thousands of natives to die. But the Spanish adventurers also brought horses to the Pueblo, and soon rival tribes were coming to steal these wonderful creatures. In the battles that followed, the homes and crops of many of the Indians were destroyed. Poorly armed, peaceful Pueblo Indians were no match for the combative Spanish or the warlike eastern Indian tribes.

EXPLORERS VENTURE WEST AND NORTH

Two Spanish missionaries who traveled through Colorado in 1776 were Padres Francisco Dominguez and Silvestre de Escalante. In his diary Dominguez wrote with enthusiasm, "We proclaimed the Gospel to [the Indians] with such happy results that they are awaiting [other] Spaniards so that they might become Christians."

In 1776 two priests journeyed through western Colorado in search of a route to the Spanish missionaries in California. They met Indians who were hunters and gatherers as well as farmers.

Thirty years later, Zebulon Pike, an army officer, led an exploration party into the region. When he sighted the 14,000-foot mountain that is now named for him, Pike proclaimed, "I believe no human being could have ascended to its pinacal [*sic*]." Today there are auto races up Pikes Peak, and a train takes visitors to the peak's pinnacle several times a day.

During the 1820s and 1830s an adventurous breed of men arrived to trap beaver. Tall hats made of beaver pelts (skins) were popular in Europe and America. Trappers could make good money selling pelts to traders, but a mountain man's life was very hard. Trapper Thomas "Broken Hand" Fitzpatrick wrote in his diary about drinking from a muddy, foul buffalo wallow when his group ran out of water: "When

Bent's Fort, a trading post of the American West, was headed by Charles Bent and Ceran St. Vrain. In 1826 they established their first post and in 1833 moved to Old Fort.

the rain falls, it is collected in these places and here the buffalo come to drink and stand during the heat of the day, adding their own excrements to the already [rotten] waters."

When the beaver hat craze petered out in the mid-1830s and most of the beaver had been trapped out, too, white men began trading with the Indians for buffalo robes and other handcrafted items. The buffalo hides were used as blankets and rugs. They set up trading posts and forts where Indians came to trade for beads and trinkets, knives and kettles, and powder and lead for their guns. Bent's Fort was a famous trading post on the Santa Fe Trail in southeastern Colorado. Today it is a national historical site near the town of La Junta. At Christmas modern-day mountain men gather at the fort to reenact an 1840s celebration.

THE UTE, ARAPAHO, AND CHEYENNE

Among the Indian peoples who made the highly prized buffalo robes were the Cheyenne. Like the Arapaho, their neighbors to the north, the Cheyenne made good use of every part of the buffalo—for food, clothing, tools, weapons, and housekeeping items. These Plains tribes lived in tepees, performed the Sun Dance, and used the sacred pipe as part of their rituals. The Sun Dance celebrated the cycle of life and death and the spiritual rebirth of people.

At the Sun Dance a young man would make a very painful sacrifice. A medicine man would make two cuts in the skin of his chest. Into them were stuck sharp pieces of wood with rope fastened to the ends. After the medicine man tied the ropes to a center pole, the boy started dancing. If he did not dance hard enough to tear the wood from his own skin, the medicine man would cut it out. The pain represented death, and the recovery from it rebirth.

In the mountains lived the Ute Indians, one of the tribes to get horses from the Spanish conquistadores. Horses made buffalo hunts in the Plains much easier and enabled the Ute to defend themselves from their enemies, the Plains Indians. Since a man's wealth was reckoned by the number of horses he owned, the Cheyenne, Arapaho, and Ute often raided each other's herds to steal them.

An even greater threat to the Ute was the white man. Before 1868 some 80 percent of what is now Colorado belonged to the Ute. By 1873 their lands measured less than one-third of the state. But the Ute weren't the only ones whose territory was shrinking. To all Colorado natives the arriving settlers were a common enemy.

With horses Ute Indians were able to access the high country of Colorado, where they hunted for deer, elk, and mountain sheep.

ROOT HOG, OR DIE

When word of the discovery of gold around Pikes Peak filtered back east in the spring of 1859, a great surge of people hit the trail for the Colorado hills. Very few of them struck it rich. The enthusiastic PIKES PEAK OR BUST! signs that the miners had painted on their wagons had to be painted over with the mournful BUSTED, BY GOSH!

The expression "Root hog, or die" was a way of saying "Work hard, or else!"

Way out up-on the Platte,— near Pikes Peak, we were told, There

by a lit-tle dig-ging, we could get a pile of gold. So we

bun-dled up our cloth-ing, re-solved at least to try, And

tempt old Mad-am For-tune, root— hog, or die.

So we traveled across the country, and we got upon the ground,
But cold weather was ahead, the first thing we found.
We built our shanties on the ground, resolved in spring to try,
To gather up the dust and slugs, root hog, or die.

Speculation is the fashion even at this early stage,
And corner lots and big hotels appear to be the rage.
The emigrants bound to come, and to greet them we will try,
Big pig, little pig, root hog, or die.

Let shouts resound, the cup pass 'round, we all came for gold,
The politicians are all gas, the speculators sold.
The "scads" are all we want, and to get them we will try,
Big pig, little pig, root hog, or die.

Surveyors now are at their work, laying off the towns,
And some will be of low degree, and some of high renown.
They don't care a jot nor little who do buy
The corner lots, or any lots, root hog, or die.

The doctors are among us, you can find them where you will,
They say their trade it is to cure, I say it is to kill;
They'll dose you and they'll physic you, until they make you so sigh,
And their powders and their lotions make you root hog, or die.

The next in turn comes lawyers, a precious set are they,
In the public dairy they drink the milk, their clients drink the whey.
A cunning set these fellows are, they'll sap you till you're dry,
And never leave you will they have to root hog, or die.

I have finished now my song, or if you please, my ditty,
And that it was not shorter is about the only pity.
And now that I have had my say, don't say I've told a lie,
For the subject I've touched will make us root hog, or die.

THE RUSH TO COLORADO

What drew these settlers to Colorado was the discovery of gold by the prospector William Green Russell and his brothers in 1858. GOLD IN KANSAS! screamed the headline in the Kansas City paper. (At the time Colorado was part of Kansas Territory.) "Every man has gold on the tongue, if none in his pocket. . . . If there is not a [decline] in this feeling before spring, our city will be depopulated."

William Larimer, a town promoter and land developer, was among the first to arrive. He founded a settlement where Cherry Creek meets the South Platte River and named it in honor of James W. Denver, governor of Kansas Territory. Doctors, shopkeepers, and businesspeople were quick to follow.

In the fall of 1859, Denver's first school opened. That same year the *Rocky Mountain News* printed its first issue. Also in 1859 a mint was established to make coins from the gold found in the area. Banks and town governments were set up in Boulder, Denver, and the Pikes Peak region, along with shops, saloons, and services of all sorts. Aunt Clara Brown, a former black slave, opened the first laundry in Central City, taking in miners' washing at her cabin. The region was growing like a prairie wildfire, and on February 28, 1861, Colorado became a territory separate from the Kansas Territory.

To haul supplies into and ore out of the mines, prospectors used ox-drawn wagons. But these were small and slow. What the infant territory needed was railroads, and during the next decade transportation pioneers like William Jackson Palmer, David Moffat, and Otto Mears scrambled to build them. Palmer's Denver & Rio Grande Western Railroad ran for more than 120 years, and Moffat's ingenious tunnel under the Continental Divide is still used by railroads today.

Central City grew out of the need for housing for gold prospectors, who flocked to the area in search of gold in nearby Gregory Gulch.

A DEATH SONG

The railroads aggravated the conflicts with Indians further. The Cheyenne chief Roman Nose spoke for all the tribes when he warned, "We will not have the wagons which make a noise [railroads] in the hunting grounds of the buffalo. If the palefaces come farther into our land, there will be scalps of your brethren in the wigwams of the Cheyennes."

By the 1860s the Plains Indians had given up so much land in treaties with the white man that they had no place left to hunt and no way to feed themselves. Government officials promised to protect the Indians and to pay them for their lands, but this rarely happened. Desperate to feed themselves, the Indians began stealing food and supplies from white settlers.

On the morning of November 29, 1864, a U.S. Army unit led by Colonel John Chivington, who was also a Methodist preacher, assaulted a settlement of peaceful Cheyenne and Arapaho. The Indians were camped at Sand Creek in southeastern Colorado, a place they had been told was under the protection of the U.S. government. During the attack White Antelope, a Cheyenne who had convinced his tribe to trust the whites, "stood in front of his lodge with his arms folded across his breast, singing the death song: 'Nothing lives long, only the earth and the mountains.'"

The Sand Creek Massacre, which killed ten army volunteers and about 150 Indians, was only one of several such battles. In the northwest mountains the Indian agent Nathan Meeker tried to make the Ute give up their way of life to become farmers. In 1879, when Meeker began to plow up the Ute's horse racetrack, they revolted, killing Meeker and his men and kidnapping the women and children at the agency. Newspaper headlines cried THE UTES MUST GO! Many Ute were

In late 1864 the Colorado militia massacred an undefended village of Cheyenne and Arapaho in an attack that is now known as the Sand Creek Massacre.

driven out of their Colorado homeland into Utah. Their descendants now live on reservations in Utah and in southwestern Colorado.

Today's Native American artists recall the past in the designs of their jewelry, in paintings, and on pottery. One of the major festivals honoring western and Indian artists is the Colorado Indian Market & Western Art Roundup, held in mid-January in Denver. There about four hundred artists gather for three days to show and sell their work. In March Native American artists and craftspeople display their works, and vendors sell native foods at the Denver powwow. Hundreds of dancers and musicians from some seventy tribes around the country come to celebrate their many cultures.

CHIEF OURAY AND CHIPETA

Ouray, whose Indian name means "Arrow," was the peace-loving chief of Colorado's Uncompahgre Ute. Unlike many Indian leaders, Ouray realized that it was useless for his people to fight the U.S. government. He worked for treaties that would benefit the Ute, traveling three times to Washington, D.C., to meet with the president.

In 1859 he married Chipeta, a Ute woman whose name means "White Singing Bird." Chipeta had a lovely voice and later learned to play the guitar. Ouray often listened to Chipeta's advice while he worked for peace with the white man. But as the government treacherously broke more and more treaties, Ouray became discouraged and angry. When people asked why he didn't fight, he said, "The agreement an Indian makes to a United States treaty is like the agreement a buffalo makes with the hunters when pierced by arrows. All he can do is lie down and give in."

When Ouray learned of the Meeker Massacre in 1879, he gave up the idea of peace and was ready to fight. Some people say it was only Chipeta's tears that made him change his mind and agree to peace. The next year, although he was very sick, Ouray made one more trip to Washington. The government wanted the Ute to sign a treaty agreeing to move to Utah. It was then that the great Ute chief made his famous statement: "I will never leave my Shining Mountains," he told American leaders. He didn't. He died in August, one month before the documents were signed forcing the Ute to move to a reservation in Utah.

The Bear Dance, during which one legend says Ouray met and fell in love with Chipeta, is still held every year. It signals the start of spring and honors the bear's strength and wisdom. In the past, people from different Ute bands would join together at the dance to feast, visit with each other, and sometimes even choose marriage partners. Even today, women ask the men to dance. They face each other in two lines that shuffle forward and back.

THE CENTENNIAL STATE

On August 1, 1876, Colorado became the thirty-eighth state. Because that was exactly one hundred years after America's independence, Colorado is called the Centennial State. Each year Coloradans celebrate August 1 as Colorado Day. But the one hundredth Colorado Day celebration, in 1976, was marred by a tragic event. On the afternoon of July 31, a thunderstorm stalled over the Big Thompson Canyon near Loveland. Twelve inches of rain poured into the canyon in just a few hours. Then raging flash floods killed 145 people in Colorado's worst natural disaster.

POPULATION GROWTH: 1870–2000

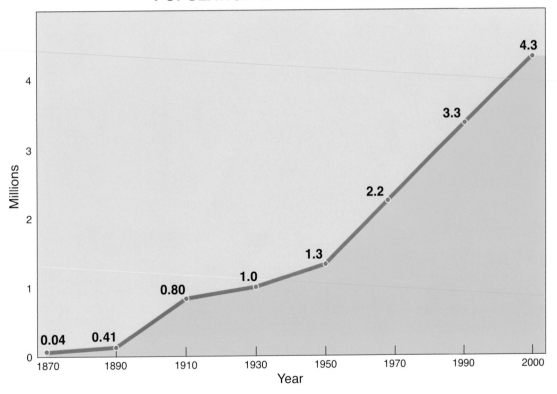

Gold, Silver, and Coal

Mining was at first the biggest business in the Centennial State, but agriculture soon took hold on the eastern plains. Pioneers learned how to raise corn, wheat, and other crops in the "Great American Desert." Some early farmers settled independently; others organized cooperative "agricultural colonies" of farmers and light manufacturers like those in Greeley and Longmont.

From 1870 to 1880, Colorado's population increased from nearly 40,000 to almost 200,000. Gold was not the only attraction. Silver lured thousands of miners to places like Aspen and Creede. In Leadville storekeeper H. A. W. Tabor became fantastically wealthy by grubstaking two poor miners. He gave them food and supplies in exchange for a share of whatever silver they found. The two struck a rich vein in the Little Pittsburgh mine, which a year later was worth $20 million.

A mining engineer in Leadville, James Joseph "J. J." Brown, became a millionaire when gold was struck in the Little Jonny mine. But it was his wife, Margaret, who became famous as the "Unsinkable Molly Brown" when she helped save passengers trapped on the *Titanic,* the ship that hit an iceberg and sank in 1912 on its first transatlantic voyage. One of the *Titanic*'s owners

The early growth and development of Colorado was spurred by miners in search of gold and silver.

cowardly tried to save himself ahead of the women and children. Yelled Molly to him, "In Leadville, Colorado, where I come from, you would be strung up on the nearest pine tree!" She helped many passengers to safety.

Leadville, like most boom towns, was "ramshackle, rough, dirty, boisterous and devil-may-care," wrote the Colorado historian Caroline Bancroft, "but remarkably honest. . . . Despite the fact that tents and cabins [the miners' homes] had no doors, there was almost no thievery." The laws were simple: no claim jumping, stealing, or murder. Anything else was okay.

Gold seeker Winfield Scott Stratton spent twenty summers looking for a strike in the southern gold fields of the Pikes Peak region. In 1891 it happened, at Cripple Creek, and overnight Stratton became one of the richest men in Colorado. Most prospectors never got that lucky.

What little they made they spent in the saloons and gambling houses. Dance hall girls like Mattie Silks and her ladies entertained the miners at night. During the day, con artists like Soapy Smith played confidence games on people, tricking them into taking chances on games that were rigged so that only Smith and his cronies would win. In the mining town of Creede, the editor of the *Chronicle* wrote in a poem, "It's day all day in the daytime, And there is no night in Creede."

At the start of the twentieth century, many Colorado men were coal miners. Most of them toiled long hours for low pay. In the hope of improving their situation, many miners began to strike. They refused to work until hours were shortened, pay was increased, or conditions in the mines were made safer. The strikes caused friction with mine owners, and in several places the National Guard was called in to bring labor disputes under control.

War and Industry

When the United States entered World War I in 1917, Colorado farmers found their products in great demand. The army needed large quantities of sugar beets, wheat, potatoes, and beans. But when the war ended in 1918 and the demand dropped, the prices of farm products fell. Suddenly, farmers found themselves unable to pay their bills, and many went bankrupt.

In the 1930s the entire country sank into the Great Depression. Many Colorado banks and businesses failed, along with others across the country. With millions of people unemployed, the government started programs to put people back to work. One of the biggest was the Civilian Conservation Corps (CCC), which trained young men to build roads and trails in national forests and to set up recreational facilities. With so much national forestland in Colorado, the CCC put more than five thousand young people to work.

In 1941, as the United States entered World War II, Colorado again played an important role. Northwest of Leadville, the army established Camp Hale to train soldiers to fight on skis. That elite group of several thousand rugged men, known as the 10th Mountain Division, later fought some grueling battles in the mountains of Italy. Toward the end of the war, as the development of the atomic bomb was under

Members of Colorado's Civilian Conservation Corps, a government-funded program to put the unemployed to work, build a mountainside trail.

way, Colorado became a primary source for two important metals: uranium and plutonium, used to create atomic explosions.

After the war the military established important bases around Colorado, among them the United States Air Force Academy, opened in 1958, and the North American Aerospace Defense Command, both near Colorado Springs. Many of the men who had trained at Camp Hale returned as civilians to Colorado's rugged mountains. They helped start an industry that has become a major source of income for the state, skiing. Resorts that today lie nestled in the Colorado Rockies are a mecca for skiers, drawn from around the world to those perfect powder runs on sunlit slopes.

Chapter Three
Living the Good Life

To see the mix of ethnic groups that make up the population of Colorado, look at a map of Denver. Such major streets as Larimer, Gilpin, and Evans were named for white settlers. Native American names appear from A to Z: Acoma to Zuni. Colorado's Hispanic heritage is remembered in street names like Tejon, Umatilla, and Santa Fe. African-American leaders from Martin Luther King Jr. to "Daddy" Bruce Randolph, the barbecue chef who fed Denver's poor and homeless each Thanksgiving, have principal Denver streets named in their honor. In downtown Denver is Sakura Square, a center for Japanese shops.

HISPANIC COLORADO TODAY

The state's oldest permanent town, San Luis, was founded in 1851 by Hispanic settlers from Mexico and Spain. The region became the center of Colorado's Hispanic culture, and these traditions are very much alive there today. Some people raise sheep, and women still weave beautiful fabrics from the wool spun from local fleece. Grandparents pass on their heritage by telling children *cuentos,* Hispanic stories or folk tales.

Colorado's population has a diverse mix of cultures, making Colorado one of the fastest-growing states in the country.

Colorado Hispanics also enjoy singing *alabados*, or ballads, Spanish folk songs that tell stories, often romantic or sad. In "Agraciada Golondrina" ("Graceful Swallow"), for example, a young man gives a letter to a swallow, asking the bird to deliver it to his girl-friend, who is far away. In three days the bird returns with a message: the young man must console himself with a birdcage, because his bird has flown away.

Hispanic Coloradans also sing *corridos*, songs the cowboys sang while they drove cattle from Texas north to Kansas or Colorado. Most, such as "El Vaquero" ("The Cowboy"), deal with hardship, violence, or tragedy:

> When we drove out toward Kansas
> With that bunch of rangy steers
> Wow! What troubles we endured
> Driving through those endless plains!

Some of the best Mexican food in the country is cooked in Colorado. Round, flat tortillas are made from flour or ground corn. Tortillas are the base for tacos, enchiladas, flautas, fajitas (say the *j* like *h*), burritos, and other delicious Mexican dishes. Chili peppers, cheese, and *frijoles refritos* (refried beans), along with big dollops of guacamole, made of avocados and seasoning, and sour cream, make great eating!

The Roman Catholic Church is the heartbeat of traditional Hispanic family life. Many churches are decorated with *santos*, paintings and statues of saints. The figures are of two types: *retablos* are pictures of the Holy Family painted on copper, canvas, wood, and tin; *bultos* are statues of religious figures carved out of wood and dressed in silk costumes. Santos are also found in many homes.

A HISPANIC *CUENTO*: THREE PIECES OF GOOD ADVICE

Long ago three poor men on the road ran into a rich man who had three bags of money. "I will give each one of you these bags," said the man, "or, I will give you three pieces of good advice." Two of the men took the money. The third took the advice:

1. Do not go down strange roads.

2. Mind your own business.

3. Look before you leap.

The men with the money headed home on a strange road that they thought would be quicker, but thieves attacked them, stole their money, and killed them. The third man stayed on the familiar road until he came to a farmhouse, where he was invited for supper. There he noticed that the farmer's wife was very, very thin, but he asked no questions. For several days he stayed and worked on the farm. When he was ready to leave, the farmer said to him, "I am very rich and I am going to give you all my money." The man was flabbergasted. "Why me?" he asked. "Because," said the farmer, "long ago I decided to feed my wife only bones and dry tortillas. I knew she could get very thin, and everyone would ask what was wrong. I made up my mind that the first person who did not ask would get all my land and money."

The delighted man rushed home, but when he looked in the window, he saw his wife kissing a priest. In a rage, he pulled out his gun, but just in time he remembered, "Look before you leap." Looking again, he realized that his wife was kissing their son, who had become a priest while the man was gone.

ETHNIC COLORADO

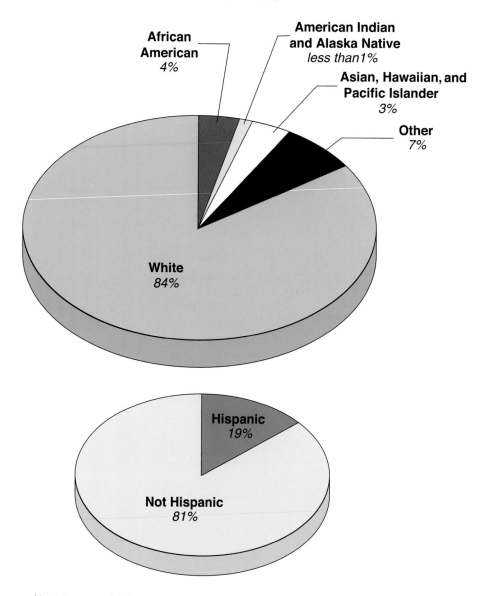

African American
4%

American Indian and Alaska Native
less than 1%

Asian, Hawaiian, and Pacific Islander
3%

Other
7%

White
84%

Hispanic
19%

Not Hispanic
81%

Note: A person of Cuban, Mexican, Puerto Rican, South or Central American, or other Spanish culture or origin, regardless of race, is defined as Hispanic.

Many Hispanic festivals, called fiestas, honor saints in the Catholic Church. At many fiestas you will find a piñata, a clay jar covered with colorful paper, usually formed into an animal shape and filled with candy and goodies. Today many piñatas are made of papier-mâché, but the fun is still the same. Children tie on blindfolds and try to hit the piñata with a stick. When it breaks, they scramble to grab the treats.

Other Hispanic holidays celebrate events from the past. On September 16, 1810, Mexicans began the war to break free of Spanish rule. Today Latinos celebrate Mexican Independence Day with parades, speeches, and the waving of Mexican flags. On May 5, 1862, Mexican soldiers won a great victory against French forces despite being out-numbered three to one. In honor of that victory, Hispanic Coloradans celebrate Cinco de Mayo with festivals, music, and food fairs. In Denver more than 120,000 people gather in Civic Center Park to enjoy food, music, and crafts. Cinco de Mayo has become much more than a Hispanic holiday. Pauline Madrid-Johnson, a festival sponsor, says, "The city of Denver is very diverse and loves the Mexican culture."

Another Hispanic event enjoyed by millions of westerners is the rodeo. *Rodeo* means "cattle roundup," for it was Mexican cowboys driving their herds into Texas who started these contests on horses. On the long cattle drives cowboys challenged each other to throw the lariat, a coiled rope, or to ride the wildest bull or horse. Today, rodeos are symbolic of the American West. Children, adults, and professional cowboys compete. Pikes Peak or Bust, the state's largest outdoor rodeo, is held in mid-August in Colorado Springs. After the professional event is the National Little Britches Rodeo for kids ages eight to eighteen. Denver's National Western, the world's largest livestock show, runs for two weeks in January and includes twenty-three rodeos.

A dancer performs a folk dance to celebrate the opening of Colorado's Cinema Latino, a theater complex catering to the Spanish-speaking audience.

For some Hispanics, however, life in Colorado is neither positive nor promising. Many Hispanic families say the education system fails their students. Dropout rates are far too high; grades and test scores are too low. Of the 30,000 Hispanic students in the Denver Public Schools, 10 percent were suspended in one recent year. Only half of all Hispanic students graduated. "There is a district-wide malaise [feeling of illness] in terms of Hispanic student achievement," said adviser Patricio Cordova.

Violence, crime, and gang warfare are major problems in some of Colorado's Hispanic communities. Rival gangs operate within the state, particularly in the Denver area. Sergeant Dennis Cribari of the Denver Police Department's gang unit said that violence is bound to result "when you get one gang going into the turf of another gang."

Today many Latinos live outside the San Luis Valley. The greatest number live in Denver, followed by Pueblo, Adams, and El Paso counties. Thirteen out of every hundred Coloradans are Hispanic, nearly 500,000 in all. Many speak both Spanish and English.

THE INDIAN INFLUENCE

Former Senator Ben Nighthorse Campbell (he served from 1992 to 2005) often got strange looks when he walked into his U.S. Senate office wearing a bolo tie and cowboy boots. Back in 1992 he rode his horse, Black Warbonnet, and wore his American Indian headdress in President Bill Clinton's first inaugural parade. Camerapeople hovered around. Why did he do it? "I wanted to let Indian people know they're not forgotten, that we're still here, we're still part of America. . . . I was trying to inspire Indian kids to be aware of it, proud of it, and not forget." Campbell is a Northern Cheyenne whose grandfather was a Sun Dance priest.

Today fewer than 1 percent of Coloradans are Native American, but Indian influence in the state is great. In addition to such county names as Kiowa and Cheyenne, mountain peaks like Uncompahgre and Tabeguache, and towns like Ouray and Saguache, Indian crafts, foods, and ways of thinking are a large part of Colorado life.

There is not as much poverty on Colorado's Indian reservations as there is on some other reservations in the nation. Oil and gas reserves on reservation lands provide income for the tribes. About 1,000 people live on the Southern Ute reservation and another 1,200 or so live on the Ute Mountain reservation. Both tribes are known for their talented

Native Americans celebrate their culture and heritage at the Ute Nation Council Tree Powwow.

craftspeople. The Sky Ute Gallery features exquisite leather and bead-work for which the Southern Ute are famous. The Ute Mountain Ute create pottery using factory-refined clay. Potters form and paint their pieces at the tribe's pottery plant, which is open for tours. Ute pottery is unique for its black-on-white design, like that of the ancient Puebloans, but each artist has a distinctive style, and every design is one of a kind.

Native American jewelers make beautiful silver pieces, often decorated with turquoise or other native stones. In their designs they use familar Indian symbols, such as thunderbirds, turtles, and salamanders.

In many Colorado supermarkets shoppers can buy Anasazi beans, the very same kind that Colorado's ancient Indians ate for supper two thousand years ago! Another popular Indian food is blue corn chips, made of corn that is actually blue. Ute tortillas are a type of round Indian flatbread with a flour base that is grilled over an open fire and served with roasted meat, fried potatoes, and green chilis.

Like their ancestors, Colorado Indians are respectful of nature and the environment. Their beliefs are reflected in legends. One legend centers around Mount Shavano, the 14,229-foot peak named for the Ute chief who remained loyal to the United States during the Ute uprising of 1879. In May and early June, when the snow is melting off the high peaks, deep crevices on the east side of Mount Shavano remain filled with snow, making the mountain look like an angel with outstretched wings. The angel is said to have been an Indian princess who misbehaved so badly that the gods turned her to ice and put her on the mountain. One year when the valley was parched by a lack of rain, the princess began to cry. Her tears (the melting snow) saved the people from drought.

CHEYENNE BATTER BREAD

Before the Cheyenne began hunting buffalo on the Great Plains, they were farmers who lived in villages and grew corn. After the Cheyenne were confined to reservations, for the first time they could bake breads and cakes in an oven. They learned to make variations on their traditional cornmeal recipes.

Serves 6

    1 quart milk or water
    2 cups yellow or white cornmeal
    3 eggs, separated
    4 tablespoons melted butter or margarine
    11/2 teaspoons salt
    1/2 teaspoon pepper

Preheat the oven to 375 degrees Fahrenheit. (Ask an adult to help you when using the oven or stove.) Bring the milk or water to a boil in a large saucepan over medium heat. Gradually stir in the cornmeal; continue stirring for a few minutes until it thickens. Remove from the heat. Separate the egg whites from the yolks, putting each into separate bowls. (This is tricky; you might want an experienced cook to help you separate the eggs.) Beat together the egg yolks, butter, salt, and pepper. Add to the cornmeal mixture. Beat the egg whites until they stand in stiff peaks. Fold the whites into the cornmeal mixture and pour into a 2-quart baking dish. Bake for 20 to 30 minutes, until the bread puffs up and turns golden brown on top. It is delicious when served warm with a dab of butter or margarine or a little honey.

FARMERS AND MINERS

Many of Colorado's white settlers were miners who came from Europe, particularly Italy, to work in the "diggings." When the gold and silver crazes were over, these immigrants found work in coal mines along the Front Range and in Routt County. For most, the dreams of striking it rich would never come true. "It was a lot of hard work and no money," said Martin Mata, who worked in the coal mines in Firestone. "We had to load two cars of rock to get one car of coal." For that, recalled Rosario Romano, miners made about three dollars for an eight-hour day.

In the late 1800s and early 1900s, German-Russian immigrants came to Colorado to homestead. These people had migrated from Germany to Russia in the early 1800s to farm new lands. Now their children and grandchildren were moving to Colorado to do the same. Immigrant Charles Boettcher brought sugar beet seeds with him from Germany. The sugar beet is grown for the sugar in its white roots. Over the years these few seeds "grew" into Great Western Sugar, one of the largest sugar companies in the nation until it was sold in 1985 and became the Western Sugar Company.

San Luis Valley farmers discovered irrigation in 1852, but it took the immigrants on the eastern plains longer to begin using the technique in raising sugar beets and potatoes. The German Russians, said the historian Robert Athearn, did more than any other group to develop farming in eastern Colorado. Another hardworking group was the Japanese immigrants, who triumphed over heat, drought, and plagues of locusts to farm the High Plains. Despite their success—or perhaps because of it—other workers resented the efficient Japanese. During World War II many Japanese Americans were seen as a threat to national security and were confined to "relocation camps" (like prisons) in Colorado and elsewhere. Despite their long history of dealing with prejudice, today Japanese own many of eastern Colorado's largest garden farms.

These large farms would not have thrived without Mexican field-workers who arrived shortly after 1900. "There was a demand for cheap, easily managed 'stoop' labor," wrote Athearn. "German Russians . . . were not the answer because they [became] growers, rather than laborers; the same was true of the Japanese." Because there were few jobs in Mexico, thousands of Mexicans came north in search of work hoeing, weeding, and harvesting the huge fields and began an enduring Hispanic presence in Colorado.

Soon the U.S. government put a limit on the number of Mexicans who could come. Still, life in the United States offered so much more hope than life in Mexico that people continue to stream across the border. Immigration is still a heated issue in Colorado today. "Many [Coloradans] recognize that there is an [illegal alien] problem and that it is growing more disturbing every day," said Congressman Tom Tancredo, former president of a research firm that studies social problems. "Colorado taxpayers must ante up tens of millions of dollars every year to provide services for aliens."

Others feel that in spite of the cost, it is wrong for the United States to close its borders. After all, they say, ours is a nation built by immigrants. Denver native Linda Chavez, president of the Center for Equal Opportunity, strongly opposes cutting the current level of legal immigration. If that happens, she said, "many immigrants who occupy [low-skilled or manual-labor] jobs will disappear from the economy, with perhaps disastrous consequences."

Many Mexicans cross the border to find work in the United States. Farmwork, such as harvesting lettuce, employs many of them in Colorado.

COWBOYS, YOUNG PROFESSIONALS, AND SKI BUMS

About 80 percent of Coloradans are Anglo, or not Hispanic, black, or Indian, with lifestyles from briefcase-carrying lawyers and oil company executives to hard-rock miners. On the eastern plains and the Western Slope are the cowboys—rough, tough, weather-beaten men and women who drive pickup trucks, wear cowboy boots and hats, and are generally conservative in their thinking. Colorado also has its share of "urban cowboys"—city dwellers who look and dress like working cowboys.

Many Colorado Anglos are single, under fifty, well educated, and career-minded. "This is a place where you can stay forever young," said thirty-nine-year-old Kirstin Karsch, a Denver attorney. "It's got everything: hiking, skiing, hot-air ballooning, water sports, nightclubs, and awesome weather. For concerts and cultural events, [there are] places like Red Rocks Amphitheater, Fiddler's Green [now known as Coors Amphitheater], and the Denver Center for the Performing Arts. Who could ask for more?"

The mountain town of Telluride attracts many of these young professionals. In late June there's the Bluegrass Festival, perhaps the finest in the country. For five full days and nights, amateur and professional bluegrass pickers perform and compete on banjos, mandolins, flat-picked guitars, and other instruments. Then in July it's jazz, performed all weekend long in Town Park. In September Telluride hosts a superb film festival.

Young singles flock to Colorado ski areas each season to "ski bum"—work where they can ski. But finding affordable housing has become a big problem in recent years. The cost of living is so high in resort towns like Aspen, Vail, and Breckenridge that service people can't afford to live there. "It was great when I worked at Eldora and lived in Boulder," recalled

Todd, a twenty-year-old ski bum. "But when I tried it at Vail, there was no way I could make ends meet."

James Michener's novel *Centennial* paints a vivid panorama of Colorado through time. Starting before the dinosaurs, the story continues into the present. Readers meet the Indian leaders Lame Beaver and Clay Basket; Pasquinel, a French *voyageur* who came to trap beaver, and his partner, Scotsman Alexander McKeag; pioneers who came west on covered wagons; ranchers and cowboys who rode the trails up from Texas. Michener's story is set in the fictional town of Centennial on the Platte River, near present-day Kersey. His research was done in libraries and museums in Denver. Said Michener, "No city could have been more pleasant to work in than Denver, except for repeated traffic tickets, the worst winter in 170 years, [and] the hottest summer in 87 [years]."

Hardworking cowboys take in a meal after a day of driving cattle at a Colorado ranch.

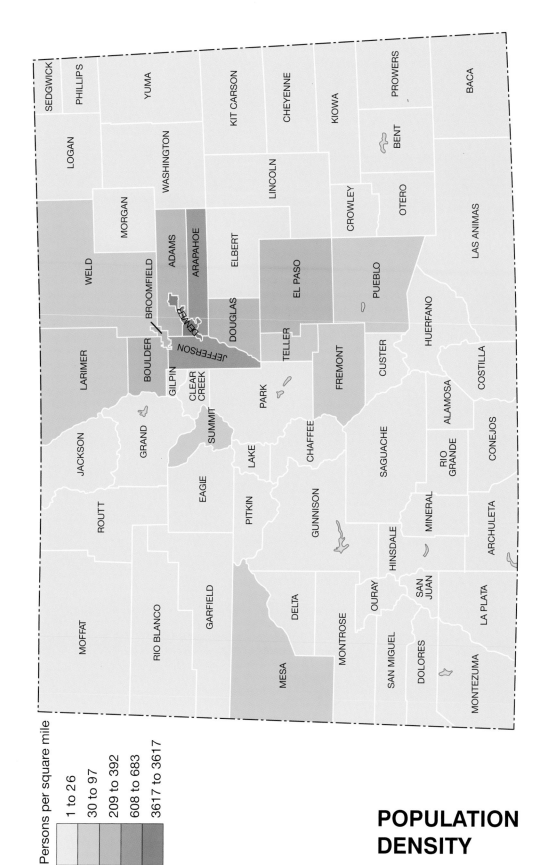

Persons per square mile

1 to 26
30 to 97
209 to 392
608 to 683
3617 to 3617

POPULATION DENSITY

THE "CALIFORNICATION" OF COLORADO

"There's a running joke in Colorado," said Leeza Williams, a school-teacher and longtime Colorado resident. "The state is getting too full of people from California!"

In recent years there has been evidence that Colorado may be becoming a victim of its own success. In the 1990s many high-tech computer companies from California, drawn by the beautiful scenery, hiking, and seemingly easier lifestyle, set up shop on Colorado's Eastern Front. Though the influx of businesses brought the state great wealth in the late 1990s, there was a downside—more people bring more development and more urban sprawl.

Through the years Colorado has enjoyed a reputation as a beautiful state with a relatively small population—a place where you can take a long hike on a summer day and feel as if you have the entire mountain to yourself. Today Colorado is being forced to confront the same problems as more populous states, like California.

"There never used to be traffic around Colorado Springs," said John Cannon, a writer. "Now what is normally a fifteen-minute drive can take an hour during rush hour."

And traffic is only part of the problem. Communities are spending more time and money making sure their towns don't become overly developed. "Developers have gotten away with murder," Dave Wilhide, an engineer, said. "They put up hundreds of houses with no sense of aesthetics. There are huge homes fifteen feet apart."

Recently the city of Boulder decided to do something about it. The city placed a ballot issue before its voters asking them to increase sales tax by 0.15 percent. The extra money would be used to maintain land the city already owned and to acquire new land that might otherwise be

As Colorado's population increases, the demand for development and urbanization grows.

lost to development. As one editorial in favor of the ballot issue put it, "Our investment in open space has defined Boulder. It has kept us from sprawling outwards, . . . provided great places for hiking, biking, horseback riding, and rock climbing."

As the population continues to increase, the people of Colorado will have to work hard to manage development so that their state retains its character and natural beauty.

CRIME AND COLUMBINE

As more people have moved to the Centennial State, Colorado has had to come to terms with growing pockets of crime. In the late 1980s Denver underwent a flurry of gang-related violence when several people were killed in downtown City Park. Denver responded by passing tough gun-control laws that made it very difficult to have a weapon within city limits. Today the parts of Denver that were associated with what became known as "the summer of violence" are slowly changing into nice neighborhoods. Such other Colorado cities as Fort Collins, Colorado Springs, and Boulder are considered to be some of the safest cities in America.

Sadly, Colorado was the setting of one of the most notorious crimes in recent American history. On April 20, 1999, students Eric Harris and Dylan Klebold walked into Columbine High School in Littleton armed with guns and bombs. Over the next few hours the two boys killed twelve students and one teacher before committing suicide. In the aftermath of the tragedy, many citizens of Colorado rallied to the cause of statewide and national gun control. At one gathering, Tom Mauser, whose teenage son had been killed, carried a sign that read MY SON DANIEL DIED AT COLUMBINE. HE'D EXPECT ME TO BE HERE TODAY. Another man, whose son was killed in a New York robbery, stated, "We have

The family of a Columbine High School murder victim prays at a remembrance service on the one-year anniversary of the tragic shootings.

standards for teddy bears. . . . But we have no safety standards for hand-guns." On the other hand, supporters of the National Rifle Association (NRA) lobbied to keep the gun laws the way they were, arguing that it is a constitutional right for an American to bear arms. Many supporters of the

NRA also pointed out that easy access to guns doesn't necessarily lead to more killings.

"In the end, the NRA won the battle," said Wendie Meade, a teacher in Colorado Springs. Indeed, though the Columbine massacre awakened a new awareness of the horror of guns in the wrong hands, there has been no significant national or statewide gun control legislation passed in the last four years.

ZERO TOLERANCE

After Columbine, school administrators everywhere were justifiably nervous about the possibility of copycat killings. One of Colorado's solutions was a zero-tolerance policy toward anyone suspected of doing something violent. "The idea is to stop a possible crime before it happens," said Margaret Szabo, a marketer in Aspen.

Though zero tolerance may have prevented some crimes, it has also gone way too far at times. Writer Rich Tosches of the *Colorado Springs Gazette* described a first grader who was suspended for having drugs. "His crime?" Tosches wrote. "He had a handful of lemon cough drops."

There was also the example of seventeen-year-old Sonya Golden, vice president of Mitchell High School's National Honor Society. She was suspended for having a 2.5 inch pocketknife in her first-aid kit . . . in the glove compartment of her car!

Chapter Four

Running the State

Government is very big in Colorado, and there are many governments . . . to be exact: 1,936! There is the federal government, the
State of Colorado, 63 counties, 267 cities and towns, 176 school
districts, and 1,428 special districts that oversee everything from
local libraries to fire departments.

—Roger Walton, legislative consultant

Both Denver and Colorado are often called "little Washington." There
are more federal government agencies there than in any other city or state
outside Washington, D.C.

Colorado sends two senators and six representatives to Congress in
Washington, D.C. Pat Schroeder, the state's first female representative,
served from 1973 to 1997. Native American Ben Nighthorse Campbell
served in the Senate from 1992 to 2005. He is a colorful personality who
rode Harley-Davidson motorcycles and wore traditional Cheyenne
Indian clothing to political events.

*Colorado's state capitol building in Denver houses the state's legislature. The gold dome
celebrates Colorado's gold rush days and the pioneers who helped build the state.*

INSIDE GOVERNMENT

The three branches of state government—the executive, legislative, and judicial—are headquartered at the capitol in Denver.

Executive

The executive branch is headed by the governor, who is elected by the people along with the lieutenant governor, secretary of state, and several other officials. Former Colorado governor Richard Lamm, known nationally for taking unpopular stands on major political issues, made an unsuccessful run for president on the Reform Party ticket in 1996. The executive branch sees that the state's laws are upheld. The laws are based on the Colorado constitution, which was adopted on July 1, 1876.

Colorado's current governor, Bill Owens, began his career in the state senate and was elected to the state's highest office in 1998. A Republican, Owens believes strongly in cutting taxes. As he put it in his State of the State address in January 2003, "We must not raise taxes. And so long as I am governor, we will not raise taxes." In his first term Owens also pushed for and saw passed an education accountability system, in which public schools are graded and forced to improve if deficiencies are found. He has also raised $15 billion to improve the state's public transportation system. Very popular, Owens was reelected in 2002 by the largest margin in Colorado history.

Legislative

The legislative branch, called the General Assembly, makes the state's laws. The General Assembly has one hundred members, sixty-five in the House of Representatives and thirty-five in the Senate. Representatives decide how the state will raise and spend its money.

Governor Bill Owens (center) celebrates his 2002 reelection with his wife, Frances (left), and Lieutenant Governor Jane Norten (right).

Judicial

The judicial branch is made up of many courts, with one or more appointed judges presiding over each. It is the job of the courts to explain the laws and make certain they uphold the Colorado constitution. When a person disagrees with the decision of a judge or jury in one court, he or she can appeal, or ask a higher court to reconsider the decision. The highest state court is the Colorado Supreme Court, made up of seven justices, one of whom is chief justice.

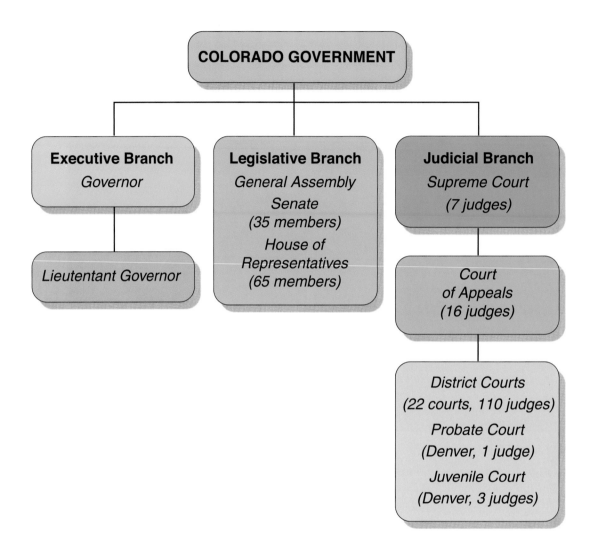

COLORADO GOVERNMENT

Executive Branch
Governor

Lieutentant Governor

Legislative Branch
General Assembly
Senate
(35 members)
House of
Representatives
(65 members)

Judicial Branch
Supreme Court
(7 judges)

Court
of Appeals
(16 judges)

District Courts
(22 courts, 110 judges)
Probate Court
(Denver, 1 judge)
Juvenile Court
(Denver, 3 judges)

COUNTY AND LOCAL GOVERNMENTS

Colorado is divided into sixty-four counties, each governed by eight elected officials and a board of at least three elected county commissioners. The commissioners appoint a county attorney. County governments handle the construction and maintenance of county roads, health and sanitation, welfare, planning and zoning, licensing, and agriculture and soil conservation.

COLORADO
BY COUNTY

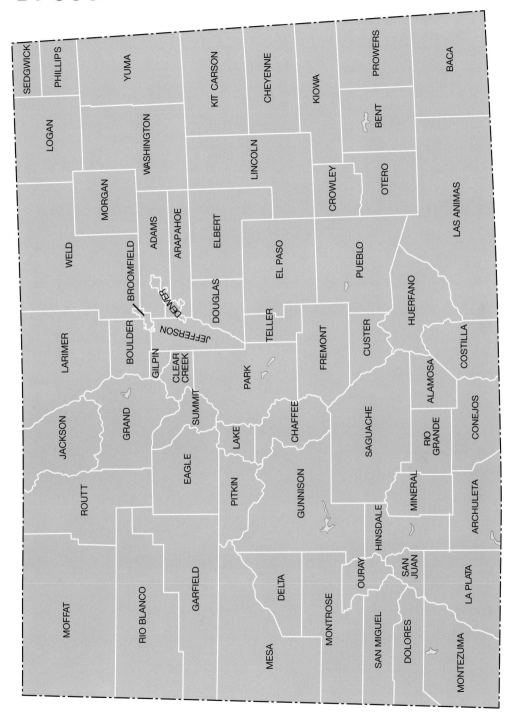

GOVERNOR VERSUS WILDLIFE

In recent years a dispute has raged in Colorado over the use and development of the state's many national parks. Though many citizens of the Centennial State want to see their parks preserved, other business interests want to throw open parklands for profitable development. In the fall of 2003, fifty-eight former Division of Wildlife employees wrote a letter to Governor Bill Owens complaining that his administration undercut their ability to protect the state's wildlife. Specifically, the letter complained about actions the governor has taken together with Greg Walcher, executive director of the Colorado Department of Natural Resources. Owens and Walcher have proposed building roads across federal lands, including national monuments and wildlife refuges. They have also called for opening parklands to off-road vehicles.

"Governor Owens and Greg Walcher are in the process of destroying some of Colorado's legacy of natural beauty forever," said Halina Cobb, a biologist.

On the other hand, Owens and Walcher feel that the environmentalists are overreacting. They claim that there are enough environmental protections in place already to keep the land safe, and that Colorado's great natural resources are there to be used as well as enjoyed by the people.

There are different forms of local governments, but towns (with two thousand or fewer residents) often have a mayor and six trustees. The trustees hire or appoint a town manager, police and fire chiefs, and staff to handle sewer and water services. Cities may have a council-manager or a mayor-council form of government. In some cities the people elect the mayor; in others the mayor is elected by the council.

Denver's government is different because the city and county are combined. The city limits are also the county limits. Denver has a mayor-council form of government.

COLORADO CITIZENS ARE CONCERNED ABOUT . . .

To vote in Colorado, a person must be at least eighteen years old and have been a resident of his or her district for at least twenty-five days. Citizens have not only a right to vote but a responsibility, too. "Democracy will not survive as a spectator sport," said government expert Roger Walton.

Forest Fires

The story goes that on June 8, 2002, U.S. Forest Service employee Terry Lynn Barton carelessly burned a letter from her estranged husband in Pike National Forest. Barton should have remembered that fires had been banned in parks due to drought conditions. The Hayman Fire was the worst forest fire in Colorado history. It burned 137,760 acres and destroyed six hundred structures before it was finally brought under control on July 18, 2003, a full year later. At her trial she was sentenced to several years in prison.

Over the past several years, Colorado has suffered a terrible drought. "We get very little rainfall," Charlie Berrin of Boulder said. "That makes the forests a tinderbox." As a result the Colorado State Parks System is extra vigilant. All visitors must restrict their campfires to designated picnic areas and fire pits. Where conditions are especially dry, fires are prohibited altogether.

Forest fires are a real threat to Colorado's forests. The state park system has created specific rules and regulations to protect the environment from damaging wildfires.

"There's not much we can do but be careful," Charlie Berrin added. "And pray for rain."

Education

Another issue of major concern is education. More and more parents are unsatisfied with the quality of Colorado's schools and with the social issues their kids face there. Because Colorado law requires that children ages seven to sixteen be educated, many parents are turning to homeschooling. When kids are schooled at home, they must be taught for at least four hours a day and study subjects determined by the state.

Charter schools, which are organized privately but operate with school district funds, are also growing in number. The charter, which states the guidelines the school must follow, must be approved by the local school board. "It's been a great alternative for us," said one parent whose child attends the Academy of Charter Schools. "The emphasis is on basics: reading, writing, math. Teachers don't spend a lot of time teaching about moral issues—things the kids should be learning at home."

School accountability reports have been instituted. Each year Colorado schools are ranked, and those that are deemed unsatisfactory are forced to improve or else receive less public money. In his 2003 State of the State address, Governor Bill Owens said, "Nearly three-quarters of the schools that received unsatisfactory ratings in 2001 have improved and moved out of that category."

Critics of the governor's program say that frequent testing in the schools inhibits creativity in the classroom. That may be true, but Governor Owens is happy with the results, asserting that Colorado now has "eleven thousand fewer students attending unsatisfactory schools than we did a year ago."

Gambling

In 1990 Colorado voters approved gambling in Central City, Black Hawk, and Cripple Creek. A special fund has been set up with a share of the gambling profits to pay for the preservation of historic sites in the state. More than forty-seven casinos are now in operation. Gambling brings nearly $500 million a year to the state. But it also brings congestion, traffic, and crime to the tiny mountain towns. In the mid-1990s, the Colorado senate approved a bill to keep children out of casinos. "I've seen children sleeping on the floor or carrying tubs of nickels for their parents," said bill sponsor Joan Johnson. The Casino Owners Association of Colorado supports the measure.

The quality of Denver's air is a concern in Colorado. Through the state's commitment to reducing pollutants, it is hoped that air quality will improve in the region.

Air Pollution

Sixth grader Valerie Martinez, like millions of other Coloradans, worries about air pollution. "When you wake up in the mornings, sometimes you can see a red fog, and that's pollution." The problem has to do with geography. The Denver metropolitan area lies beside the Rocky Mountains, which block wind currents and trap the brown cloud of smog in the city.

Clean Air Colorado is an agency that educates people about air pollution. It also tests cars to see if their emissions are causing pollution. During the high pollution season (November 1 through March 31) Clean Air Colorado issues air quality reports twice a day. A blue pollution advisory means that the air quality is good. A red advisory means poor air, so Denver metro residents cannot burn wood in stoves or fireplaces and should limit their driving. In recent years Colorado's air has received better ratings.

"Who knows?" asked reporter Rick Jones. "Hopefully, the famous brown cloud will soon be history."

THE FIGHT FOR WATER

The biggest problem facing Colorado today is something that most Americans may take for granted—water. On the heels of four years of severe drought, Colorado is running out of this most vital natural resource. Reporter Bill McKeown of the *Colorado Springs Gazette* put it like this: "With only fifteen inches of rain a year, our state gets our water solely from snow melt. On top of that, no rivers run into Colorado. All the water that is here runs out into other western states."

With some cities enacting restrictions on how often citizens can water their lawns, the government is getting involved. In 2003 the people of Colorado voted on Referendum A, a law that aimed to raise $2 billion to be devoted to water storage projects. In the days leading to the vote, the debate was fierce and largely split down regional lines: While most of the state's water is in the western part of the state, most of the people live in the cities of the Eastern Front. As a result many citizens in the west did not support the referendum, fearing that the east would take too much of their water and dry up their rivers and ponds. Many Colorado environmentalists also stood against the bill. They argued that 85 percent of the state's water is used by agriculture and that the farmers should do a better job conserving it. Then there were other citizens who didn't trust Governor Owens to do the right thing with the money if the bill passed. Not surprisingly, many easterners—the people who desperately need the water—favored the bill.

In the end Referendum A was easily defeated. One reason had to do with the way the bill was written. As the reporter Kyle Henley said, "Most Coloradans won't vote for a measure that includes money unless there are specifics about how that money will be spent." Since the referendum didn't say what exact water projects the $2 billion would be spent on, many voters said no.

The U.S. Secretary of the Interior, Gale Norton, brokered a deal in 2003 in which California agreed to use less of Colorado's water. Still, the people of Colorado need to figure out a way to catch and store the water they have. Until then, most citizens of the Centennial State are keeping their fingers crossed that there isn't another drought.

Water conservation in Colorado is a large issue facing the state's lawmakers. Colorado farmers use a large percentage of the state's water for irrigating their fields.

Chapter Five

How Coloradans Earn a Living

Colorado provides its citizens with lots of different ways to make a living. Though tourism and agriculture have been the state's bedrock industries, mining, technology, and military activites have also thrived in the Centennial State. In the late 1990s the state enjoyed huge economic growth. The Corporation for Enterprise Development awarded Colorado straight A's for economic performance, business vitality, and development capacity. Colorado took advantage of the "tech boom," attracting many companies in the computer industry. With so much money pouring into the state, Colorado citizens were able to take advantage of the surging stock market. Office and home construction skyrocketed. The government got into the act, too, building a huge new airport, a library, and three sports arenas in Denver alone.

With the influx of people, such industries as construction provide employment for steelworkers, carpenters, and electricians, just to name a few.

But as the national economy faltered at the start of the twenty-first century, so did Colorado's. After the building surge in the 1990s, no more new homes were needed. As a result, the construction industry lost over ten thousand jobs. Worse, with the collapse of the tech bubble, Colorado's computer industry lost 30,000 jobs. Colorado's tourism industry also took a hit of ten thousand jobs because of drought and a surge in forest fires.

"It's been a rough couple of years," said Tom Brown, a builder in Colorado Springs. "But Colorado is unique. Our economy is usually solid. Things always turn around."

COLORADO WORKFORCE

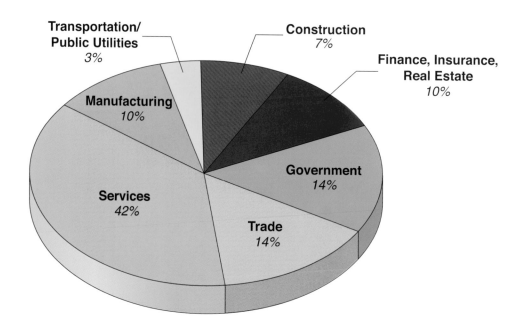

Transportation/Public Utilities 3%

Construction 7%

Finance, Insurance, Real Estate 10%

Manufacturing 10%

Government 14%

Services 42%

Trade 14%

MINING

Mining is an important part of Colorado's economy. After World War II, when the demand for oil increased, companies began drilling in eastern Colorado and processing oil shale on the Western Slope. Then, as nuclear energy came into wider use, energy companies required uranium. The extensive mining of it left a legacy of uranium pollution in Colorado's rivers. Nearly three-fourths of the world's molybdenum (ma-LIB-den-um) is mined in Colorado. "Moly" is used with iron to make high-speed cutting tools.

AGRICULTURE

Many Coloradans are employed in farming and ranching. Field crops like grains, beans, corn, hay, wheat, and potatoes create most of the agricultural income for Colorado. Nearly every potato raised in Weld, the largest agricultural county, is made into potato chips.

Onions are Colorado's biggest small-farm vegetable crop. A "best" product is the incredibly sweet, juicy cantaloupes raised near Rocky Ford in southeastern Colorado. The town, which calls itself the nation's melon capital, claims that 95 percent of the world's cantaloupe seed is grown on its farms.

Though not a major employment sector in Colorado, agriculture employs workers who plant and harvest crops, such as potatoes.

Brilliant sunshine and mild temperatures make Colorado a major supplier of carnations. Greenhouses—of which there are fewer and fewer as the cost of natural gas rises—produce carnations in brilliant colors that stay fresh for weeks after being cut.

Sheep and cattle are the most common Colorado livestock, raised on ranches in the eastern plains or in the mountain parks. Stockmen operate feedlots, where the animals are taken to be fattened before they are slaughtered. In fact, Colorado has more sheep and lamb in feedlots

There are over 225,000 sheep in the state of Colorado. The livestock industry is an important source of employment.

MILITARY MONEY

Colorado's economy has been helped throughout the years because the state is home to many military bases. In 2001 the military establishment poured $2.67 billion into the five installations around Colorado Springs, spending money on payroll, contracts, and services. These five bases had a whopping 41,672 employees—the most of any business sector in the city.

All in all, the military accounts for about 35 percent of the Colorado Springs economy. Local economist David Bamberger said, "Put it this way: One out of every three people employed here is employed as a military person or as a person directly supported by defense dollars."

With the country at war with Iraq, Coloradans can probably expect federal military spending to remain steady for the foreseeable future.

than any other state and is one of the biggest cattle feeders in the United States.

If you like turkey bologna or turkey hot dogs, you can thank the big birds raised in Colorado. Some do end up on Thanksgiving platters, but many more are shipped to food-processing companies to be packaged with other meat forms, such as ham or hamburger.

TECHNOLOGY

In the mid-1990s Colorado's Front Range became a high-tech center. Computer giants like Hewlett-Packard, Storage Technology, IBM, and Digital Equipment Corporation opened national or regional headquarters there. "Programming, data processing and other related services—including software—are on a roll," reported the *Denver Post* at the time.

Big companies are attracted to Colorado partly because it's a beautiful place to live and work. "We'd been here as plain old postcard-buying tourists," recalled the wife of a U.S. West employee. "When my husband had the chance to transfer here, we couldn't believe it. It didn't take long to say yes."

The tech boom of the late 1990s fueled Colorado's amazing economic growth. Unfortunately, no other industry's profits dropped as quickly in the wake of the recession at the beginning of the twenty-first century.

"Some companies are closing up shop," said Michael LeBow, a software engineer in Denver. "Other jobs are being lost to workers overseas in places like India."

The bust of the tech-sector bubble has hurt Denver and Colorado Springs in particular—cities that benefited enormously from business

THE ECONOMY OF WILDLIFE

When a citizen of Colorado or a tourist buys a pair of binoculars to watch a herd of bighorn sheep grazing near route I-70, he or she is helping the Colorado economy. According to a study by the Colorado Division of Wildlife, in 2003 over 1.5 million people spent $624.4 million observing wildlife.

Much of the money was spent by tourists on rental cars, hotels, and restaurants. Other purchases included cameras, film, backpacks, and winter clothes. All of this is good news for the Centennial State, especially for the poorer, rural areas that have most of the wildlife. Economist Richard Sales put it this way: "Colorado is a prime example of how protecting the environment and wildlife can help the state's citizens earn a living."

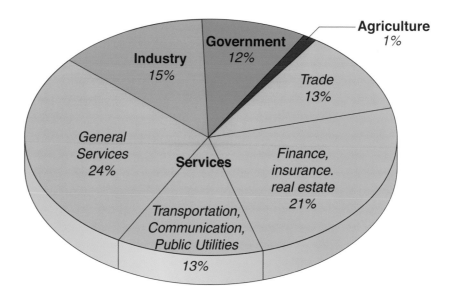

2002 GROSS STATE PRODUCT: $180 Million

Government 12%

Industry 15%

Agriculture 1%

Trade 13%

General Services 24%

Services

Finance, insurance. real estate 21%

Transportation, Communication, Public Utilities 13%

investment in the 1990s. Luckily for the people of Colorado, the computer age is here to stay. As the national economy improves, tech businesses will continue to be a large and important part of Colorado's economy.

TOURISM

With all its natural beauty, it's not surprising that tourism is one of the top-ten industries in Colorado. About 8 percent of Colorado's citizens work in tourist-related fields, serving the 20 million or more travelers who visit Colorado each year. Many come in the summer to hike or camp in the mountains. But the big-money attraction is skiing. Resorts like Breckenridge, Keystone, Steamboat Springs, and Winter Park attract more than 10 million people each year. Respondents to a *Skiing* magazine survey of favorite ski resorts worldwide chose Colorado for three of the

Colorado ski resorts, drawing more than 10 million visitors each year, must hire a workforce to accommodate and serve their visitors.

top ten: Vail, Aspen, and Telluride. "Aspen is a place," wrote the *Skiing* columnist Hollis Brooks, "where most people ski to be seen." Not all resorts are so fashion conscious. Vail is a place for all ages, "like a big city compris[ed] of many neighborhoods that you can sample day by day," said one visitor. The cowboy ski town of Steamboat Springs is "down-home, all-American, blue jeans friendly," wrote *Skiing*'s Eric Hanson. "Cowboy hats and boots are as common as powder suits and ski boots. . . . The mountain itself is about as kid-friendly as you can get."

In addition to the best skiing in North America, Colorado ski resorts sponsor special events to lure tourists. For example, each January, Breckenridge hosts the Ullr Fest and World Cup Freestyle in honor of Ull, the Norse god of winter. Along with a parade and fireworks, there are Nordic events and a freestyle skiing competition with some of the world's best skiers.

The Steamboat Springs Winter Carnival runs for a week in February and features ice-sculpture competitions, a hockey tournament, and ski jumping. There's also a race in which riders sit on shovels and are pulled by horses through the streets. The high school band marches on skis, and at night a "lighted man" skis down nearby Howelsen Hill. The scene is similar at Winterskol, where fireworks and torchlit runs draw onlookers out into the night at Snowmass and Aspen.

"Colorado's mountains are the best in the country," said Loveland ski instructor Shawn O'Hara. "I've taught at a bunch of areas. You'll never find anything like the superb powder, the high-altitude sun, the gorgeous blue sky, and the friendly, laid-back people in this state."

Like every other industry in the state, tourism took a big hit in the early years of the twenty-first century. Many journals and newspapers attribute the drop in tourism to several factors. "The attacks on

EARNING A LIVING

Natural Resources

U	Uranium
V	Vanadium
Z	Zinc
	Petroleum
S	Silver
	Sand, gravel
L	Lead
M	Molybdenum
	Natural gas
C	Coal
	Copper
G	Gold

Manufacturing

- Electrical & electronic goods
- Food processing
- Heavy machinery
- Metal products
- Transportation equipment

Agriculture

- Barley
- Beans
- Beef Cattle
- Corn
- Hay
- Poultry
- Sheep
- Sugar beets
- Vegetables
- Wheat

September 11 were probably number one," said Jane Abernethy, an Aspen lawyer. "The economy crashed, and people were scared to fly."

Many would-be tourists also stayed out of the state while brave firefighters tried their best to bring the immense Hayman forest fire under control. On top of everything, Colorado suffered a few years in a row of meager snowfall. "We've had some bad luck," continued Abernethy. "Things out of our control that have kept people out of the state. But things are turning around. We have one of the most beautiful places in the world. And people will come back."

LOOKING AHEAD

One way to measure the status of a state's economy is to look at its population growth. During the 1990s, when times were good, Colorado was gaining about 70,000 people a year—most moving to the Centennial State in search of jobs. But as jobs became scarce, the number fell sharply. Still, there is cause for optimism. Most economists forecast an annual population growth of 40,000 people over the next few years. At the same time unemployment—which stood at about 5 percent in 2004, slightly below the national average—is expected to drop.

"It seems pretty clear that the economy has bottomed out," said reporter Kyle Henley. "Things are beginning to look up."

After weathering a tough economic patch, state revenues are increasing for the first time in three years. As conditions improve and more jobs are created, Colorado citizens and politicians are trying to figure out the best ways to plan for their state's future.

"A solid or sustainable economy is not just based on jobs," wrote Elizabeth Garner in a paper on Colorado's economy.

Indeed, to plan successfully for the future, Colorado has to make some important choices. How much land should be developed? How much should citizens be taxed? Which regions in the state should get more aid than others? How should water storage be improved?

These are all challenging issues. But blessed with hardworking citizens and some of the most stunning scenery in the country, the Centennial State is sure to have a glorious future.

The future of Colorado's growth is supported by Coloradans who believe in the state's equal opportunities, communities, and natural environment.

Chapter Six

The Grand Circle Tour

Snowy mountain peaks, silvery mountain streams, peaceful shimmering lakes, incomparable camping grounds . . . all combine to place [Colorado] at the very front among tourist lands of the country.
—from *Colorado for the Tourist*, 1912

Little has changed since the guidebook *Colorado for the Tourist* was written in 1912. Visitors flying into Denver International Airport today are greeted by beautifully engineered imitation snowy mountain peaks that form the roof of the terminal building. This major airport covers a land area of fifty-three square miles! From the terminal, arriving passengers have a dramatic view of the Colorado Rockies and the skyline of downtown Denver. Let's begin our Grand Circle tour right there.

GOING DOWNTOWN

The birthplace of Denver, the Mile High City, is near the spot where Cherry Creek and the Platte River meet. Denver has many attractions. The Forney Transportation Museum is the place for you if you like things

With the Rocky Mountains as a backdrop, Denver is one of the most visited cities in the United States, offering cultural and natural wonders alike.

with wheels. The aviation heroine Amelia Earhart's roadster is there, as is the world's largest steam locomotive, a bicycle built for four, Prince Aly Khan's Rolls-Royce Phantom I, and hundreds of other unique vehicles.

At KidSlope, run by the Children's Museum of Denver, you can learn to ski on plastic "snow," winter or summer. For kids who like to work with tools, the museum has an irresistible woodworking shop. If science experiments are your thing, there's a lab filled with wires and batteries, chemicals, magnets, and other items. Budding movie directors and computer buffs will find a light room, sound room, and computer lab. There's truly something for everyone.

On a hill overlooking downtown Denver sits Colorado's gold-domed capitol, the real gold leaf donated by proud Colorado miners when the building was under construction. The fifteenth step of the long granite stairway leading up to the entrance marks the spot that is exactly 5,280 feet, or one mile, above sea level. Later measurements proved that to be wrong, so a brass plaque was installed on the eighteenth step saying that that is truly the one-mile level. Now the information is carved into the step. Inside the capitol, visitors can climb up into the gold dome. But signs warn those who are out of shape that there are ninety-three steps, and it's harder to breathe in high-altitude country!

Across Civic Park from the capitol is the U.S. Mint. Half of all coins in the United States are manufactured there—40 million coins a day, worth approximately $1.5 million. That's 5 billion coins a year! The Denver mint holds the largest supply of gold in the United States outside of Fort Knox, Kentucky.

Nearby is the Colorado History Museum, featuring exhibits on Native Americans, the gold rush, ancient cultures, and many interesting periods and events in Colorado's history.

Built in 1886, the capitol building is modeled after the U.S. Capitol Building in Washington, D.C. Its dome is covered with 200 ounces of 24-carat gold leaf.

THE BOULDER MOUNTAIN AREA

Boulder is home to the University of Colorado Buffalos, one of college football's finest teams. But football isn't the only athletic event in this city. The 10K Bolder Boulder attracts some 35,000 running enthusiasts to Colorado each year on Memorial Day. Boulder is a liberal city, where almost anything goes—except smoking. Most Boulderites are very health and fitness conscious, and the city council voted for a citywide ban on smoking.

Heading up Boulder Canyon, massive rock formations tower over both sides of the road, just a few feet from your car. Even if you strain your neck by the window, there are many spots where you can't see the tops of the rocks. As you travel along the steep curves and narrow switchbacks of Colorado's canyon roads, it becomes clear why these are called the Rocky Mountains.

Boulder Canyon takes travelers to the quaint town of Central City, once a mining town but now a gambling center. On the floor of the Teller House is painted a picture of a mysterious woman named Madeline. Done by the wandering artist Herndon Davis in 1934, this is "The Face on the Barroom Floor." The nearby Central City Opera House, still sporting some of its brass, wood, and red velvet decor from the late 1800s, offers excellent performances every summer.

The Peak to Peak Highway leads north from Central City to Estes Park, a gateway to Rocky Mountain National Park. The scenery there is breathtaking, with more than one hundred peaks reaching ten thousand feet or higher. One of the nicest short hikes in the park is around Bear Lake where, on most days, you can see a spectacular reflection of Hallett Peak in the crystal blue water. Take a picnic lunch, even in winter, as long as the sun is out to keep you warm. But watch out for gray jays, called camp robbers, who will sweep down and grab your sandwich.

Once an old mining town, Central City is now a tourist destination full of casinos.

Bear Lake in Rocky Mountain National Park is a favorite destination for hikers.

If you're lucky, you may spot a mountain goat, bear, moose, or mule deer. Spring and fall are the best times to see elk and bighorn sheep, for when there's snow in the high country, they move lower to find food. One of the most common of the 250 species of birds in the park is the Stellar's jay, a gorgeous creature with a long crest on its black head, white markings on its face, and a blue body and tail.

Trail Ridge Road, the main route through the park, is the world's highest continuous paved highway. Snow, high winds, and poor visibility close the road from October to May, but during the summer travelers can cross the Continental Divide into the town of Grand Lake. Colorado's largest natural lake has the highest-altitude yacht dock in America and is a popular sailing and fishing spot.

Along the way you'll see a parade of wildflowers—some nine hundred varieties grow in the park. Among them, you're sure to spot the blue columbine, Colorado's state flower, in groves of aspens—trees that shimmer a gorgeous gold when their leaves turn in the fall.

THE COLORADO TRAIL

To explore Colorado by foot, the best route is along the Colorado Trail (CT), a wilderness path running northeast to southwest across the state between Denver and Durango. The CT is one of the most beautiful hikes in America, stretching 469 miles through Colorado's magnificent mountains. "The Colorado Trail," says the *Backpacker* magazine editor Tom Shealey, "will take you places, both within and without."

Don't worry. You don't have to be an "end to ender" to enjoy the CT. There are many day hikes that are not rugged or grueling but offer the same spectacular scenery. If you do decide to tackle the entire trail, you'll pass through seven national forests, six wilderness areas, cross or parallel five major river systems, and pass through eight mountain ranges.

The building of the trail was undertaken by Gudy Gaskill, called the Mother of the Colorado Trail, and before it was completed in 1973, more than three thousand teenage and adult volunteers had notched trees, moved or marked rocks, carved pathways, and moved dirt. Their help reduced the cost of building the trail from $8,000 a mile to only $500 a mile—and most volunteers recount that they had a wonderful time doing it!

PLACES TO SEE

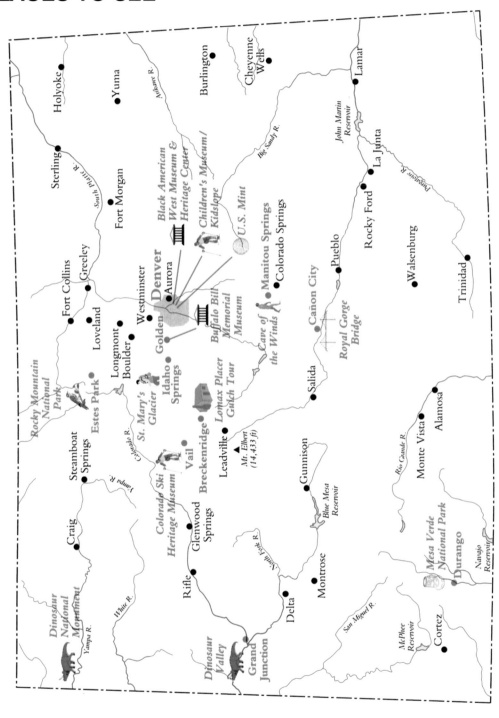

COLORADO SPRINGS AND SOUTH

Another high-altitude road trip is to the top of Pikes Peak, a trek made by thousands of tourists each year. The Pikes Peak Hill Climb in mid-July is the second-oldest auto race in America. Big-name drivers like Al Unser and Mario Andretti compete in the "Race to the Clouds." The Manitou & Pikes Peak Railway carries sightseers to the top of the mountain.

The Colorado Springs area is filled with interesting spots. Young cowboys and cowgirls should visit the ProRodeo Hall of Fame and Museum of the American Cowboy. There you can practice lassoing an iron bull's head; see exhibits of saddles, boots, cowboy hats, and other gear; and watch a variety of films about cowboys and rodeos.

Near Manitou Springs is Cave of the Winds, a real cave filled with colored lights that illuminate the striking formations. There are also paved pathways wide enough for a baby stroller. Those looking for a more realistic outdoor experience should visit the 1,350-acre Garden of the Gods park. Elephant Rock (you can actually see its trunk) and Balanced Rock (one on top of the other) are among the massive red sandstone formations. Near the park is the Manitou Cliff Dwellings Museum, a village of homes modeled after the famed Anasazi pueblos. The homes were built in 1907 with stones salvaged from actual Indian dwellings. Since these are replicas, people are allowed to climb on and explore the "ruins."

South of Manitou Springs at Florissant Fossil Beds National Monument, volcanic ash has preserved a 35- to 40-million-year-old rain forest. The Petrified Forest Loop, a mile-long hiking trail, takes visitors to Big Stump, the remains of an ancient giant sequoia tree. South of Florissant is Cripple Creek, once called "the World's Greatest Gold Camp," which today is a gambling center. To relive the mining days, tour

Garden of the Gods is home to 300-million-year-old red sandstone rock formations worn by centuries of erosion.

the one-thousand-foot-deep Mollie Kathleen Mine, which operated until the early 1960s.

Spectacular Royal Gorge, near Cañon City west of Pueblo, was carved nearly 3 million years ago by the Arkansas River. Rock walls rise 1,053 feet up the sides of this awesome canyon. Winding along the bottom on the narrow bank is the track of the Southern Pacific Railway. Spanning the top of the gorge is the world's highest suspension bridge, built in 1929. The world's steepest incline railway takes visitors to the bottom of "Royal Gorgeous" in an elevator-like cage.

Listed on the National Register of Historic Places, the Royal Gorge Bridge is more than one-quarter of a mile long, hangs 1,053 feet above the Arkansas River, and is the world's highest suspension bridge.

SEEING COLORADO BY TRAIN

Amtrak's California Zephyr runs east/west across the state. The ride from Denver west to Grand Junction passes through more than two hundred miles of the grandest scenery anywhere in the United States. Soon after leaving Denver, the train begins a slow, steep climb to the Continental Divide, passing through twenty-eight tunnels that burrow through huge spires of rock.

After emerging at Winter Park ski area on the west side of the 6.2-mile Moffat Tunnel, the train heads across broad, flat North Park, where ranching is a major business. Near Granby the track joins the Colorado River, and the two run somewhat parallel throughout the rest of the trip.

The first of the river's spectacular canyons is just east of Glenwood Springs. This spa and resort town is home to the world's largest outdoor hot springs mineral pool. The swimming pool, as long as two city blocks, averages 90 degrees Fahrenheit. The smaller therapy pool is kept at 104 degrees Fahrenheit. Glenwood Springs is the birthplace of the teddy bear. President Theodore (Teddy) Roosevelt, who loved to hunt, stayed at the elegant Hotel Colorado while visiting the Rockies. One legend says that after one unsuccessful expedition, a chambermaid felt sorry for him and made a stuffed bear that his daughter named "Teddy's bear." Another story says that a cartoonist made a drawing showing a bear cub Roosevelt spared while hunting.

West of Glenwood Springs, passengers head through beautiful Byers Canyon near Hot Sulphur Springs. The town was named for the rich mineral springs located there. Farther west is gorgeous Gore Canyon, with its picture-book spires of rock rising steeply on either side of the river. Beyond that, heading into the plateau region, the train passes through oil shale and Book Cliff country. The Book Cliffs are sandstone formations shaped exactly like their name. To the south in the distance is Grand Mesa, the world's largest flattop mountain.

The Hot Springs Pool Complex in Glenwood Springs is almost two blocks long. First used by the Ute Indians, the springs have been used by presidents, royalty, and celebrities.

Ahead lies Grand Junction, named because it is the meeting point of the Colorado (formerly the Grand) and the Gunnison rivers. Just west of the city is Colorado National Monument, a fairyland of deep canyons and natural rock sculptures with fanciful names like Praying Hands and Kissing Couple. The explorer John Otto wrote in the early 1900s, "I came here last year and found these canyons, and they felt like the heart of the world to me."

FUN-FILLED COLORADO FAIRS

The "Fun and Only" Colorado State Fair has been held in Pueblo every August since 1872. Today it draws more than a million visitors a year, making it the thirteenth-largest state fair in the nation. During the fair's eleven days there are three parades and seven days of rodeos sponsored by the Professional Rodeo Cowboys Association. The fair has all kinds of high-tech exhibits and agricultural displays with western themes. The small-animal competition includes the world's largest rabbit show. There's also a stock show, a fiesta, world-class carnival rides, and contests for kids in bubblegum blowing and melon racing. The fair also offers big-name entertainment, usually by country-western musicians.

The city of Denver also hosts two large fairs. In June is the Capitol Hill People's Fair. The thirty-year-old event draws over 250,000 visitors, who stroll among the six hundred or more booths that offer everything from exotic food to intricate crafts to advice on sewing or politics. The Festival of Mountain and Plain has been held in Denver since 1895. Its main attraction is the Taste of Colorado, where some of the finest restaurants give out free samples from their menus.

TEN LARGEST CITIES

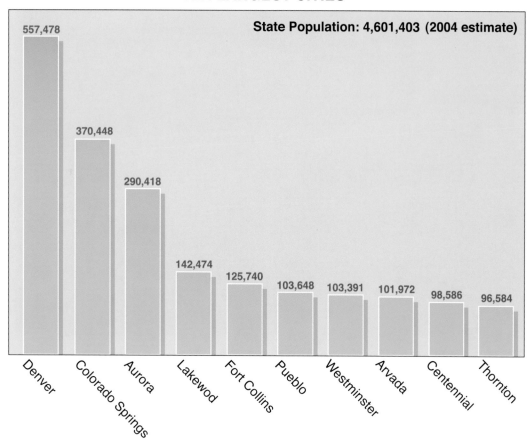

State Population: 4,601,403 (2004 estimate)

City	Population
Denver	557,478
Colorado Springs	370,448
Aurora	290,418
Lakewood	142,474
Fort Collins	125,740
Pueblo	103,648
Westminster	103,391
Arvada	101,972
Centennial	98,586
Thornton	96,584

SOUTHWEST BY CAR

From Grand Junction our Grand Circle Tour heads south by car along the beautiful Dolores River to the southwestern corner of the state. There lies Mesa Verde National Park, where the ancient Anasazi ruins and cliff dwellings are preserved. From nearby Durango, travelers can ride on an 1880s narrow-gauge steam train. The Durango & Silverton Narrow Gauge Railroad carries passengers round-trip through the mountains to the quaint old mining town of Silverton.

Hikers venture in the Great Sand Dunes National Monument, the tallest dunes in the United States.

Our return to the east takes us near Great Sand Dunes National Monument. These dunes are mountains of sand rising to peaks about seven hundred feet high and covering a strip thirty-nine miles long. They were formed when eroding rock and sediment, tossed by the constant southwest winds, settled at the base of the Sangre de Cristo (Blood of Christ) Mountains. Children love to ride sheets of cardboard down these sand mountains or "ski" downhill on their bare feet.

The road north from the Sand Dunes winds through Colorado's highest mountains. Among the giants are the Collegiate Peaks: Yale, Princeton, Harvard, Columbia, and Oxford—all of them towering above 14,000 feet—and the state's highest at 14,433 feet, Mount Elbert. The nearby city of Buena Vista on the Arkansas River claims to be the white-water rafting capital of the world.

Farther north is Fairplay, just eighteen miles from the geographic center of Colorado and the center of the South Park gold rush in 1859. Today a restoration of South Park City (Fairplay's original name) includes stores, offices, saloons, a school, and homes just as they were in the gold rush days.

From Fairplay our tour heads back toward Denver through Golden. At the Colorado School of Mines in Golden is the National Earthquake Information Center. When an earthquake occurs anywhere in the world, the center transmits information by computer to scientists and agencies worldwide. If you like trains, stop at the Colorado Railroad Museum, where more than fifty locomotives, railway cars, and other railroad items are on display.

For a hair-raising ride, a beautiful view, an interesting museum, and a close-up look at hang gliders, drive up Lookout Mountain near Golden. More than half a million people make the trip each year to catch this breathtaking view of the Great Plains. At the top is the grave of Buffalo Bill (William F. Cody) and the Buffalo Bill Memorial Museum, which houses all sorts of objects from Buffalo Bill's Wild West performances.

The return to Denver completes our Grand Circle tour of Colorado. But for every interesting stop, there are dozens more that were not made. We could have visited the Mountain Bike Hall of Fame in Crested Butte or ridden the Platte Valley Trolley in Denver. We might have viewed the Living Trees in Sterling, where sculptors have carved trunks to look like giraffes and other objects. On a February tour we could have stopped in Loveland to get our valentines stamped with a special postmark from "Love Land." But don't despair. Your stamped valentines will be canceled for you if you send them in an envelope to the main Loveland post office. For all the other great sights and more, however, you'll have to make another trip to the Centennial State.

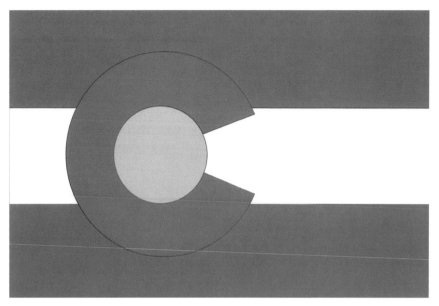

THE FLAG: The state flag has three bands running horizontally. The top and bottom bands are blue for blue skies, and the middle band is white for snow. A large red (for the reddish soil) C for Colorado surrounds a golden disk representing the sun. The flag was adopted in 1911.

THE SEAL: The Colorado state seal has a shield whose top part has three snowcapped mountains with clouds above. The bottom part shows a miner's pick and mallet. Above the shield is the eye of God inside a pyramid and a Roman fasces, a bundle of sticks surrounding an ax. The fasces represents the republican form of government. Below the shield is the state motto written in Latin, Nothing without Providence. The seal was adopted in 1877.

State Survey

Statehood: August 1, 1876

Origin of Name: Colorado takes its name from the Colorado River. The river was named for the red canyons through which it flows. *Colorado* is a Spanish word meaning "color red."

Nickname: Centennial State

Capital: Denver

Motto: Nothing without Providence

Bird: Lark bunting

Animal: Rocky Mountain bighorn sheep

Flower: Rocky Mountain columbine

Tree: Colorado blue spruce

Gem: Aquamarine

Fossil: Stegosaurus

Rocky Mountain bighorn ram

GEOGRAPHY

Highest Point: 14,433 feet above sea level at Mount Elbert

Lowest Point: Arikaree River (3,315 feet above sea level)

Area: 104,091 square miles

Greatest Distance North to South: 276 miles

Greatest Distance East to West: 387 miles

Bordering States: Wyoming and Nebraska to the north, Oklahoma and New Mexico to the south, Nebraska and Kansas to the east, and Utah to the west

Hottest Recorded Temperature: 118 degrees Fahrenheit at Bennett on July 11, 1888

Coldest Recorded Temperature: –61 degrees Fahrenheit at Maybell on February 1, 1985

Average Annual Precipitation: 15 inches

Major Rivers: Animas, Arkansas, Blue, Colorado, Dolores, Gunnison, North Platte, Republican, Rio Grande, San Juan, South Platte, White, Yampa

Major Lakes: Blue Mesa, Dillon, Granby, Grand, McPhee, Meredith, Pueblo, Shadow Mountain, Summit

Trees: ash, aspen, blue spruce, cottonwood, Douglas fir, Engelmann spruce, juniper, maple, oak, piñon pine, ponderosa pine

Wild Plants: buttercup, cactus, columbine, daisy, forget-me-not, greasewood, Indian paintbrush, larkspur, mountain lily, pasqueflower, prickly poppy, orchid, sagebrush, violet, wild geranium, wild iris, wild rose, yucca

Blue Columbine

Animals: antelope, beaver, black bear, bobcat, coyote, elk, fox, jackrabbit, marmot, marten, mountain goat, mountain lion, mule deer, pika, prairie dog, Rocky Mountain bighorn sheep, skunk

Birds: bald eagle, bluebird, blue jay, brown thrasher, duck, grouse, hermit thrush, lark bunting, meadowlark, mountain chickadee, mourning dove, oriole, peregrine falcon, pheasant, prairie chicken, quail, Rocky Mountain jay

Fish: bass, bluegill, catfish, crappie, perch, salmon, sunfish, trout

Endangered Animals: bald eagle, bonytail minnow, gray wolf, greater prairie chicken, greater sandhill crane, greenback cutthroat trout, grizzly bear, humpback drub, lynx, peregrine falcon, piping plover, razorback sucker, river otter, Uncompahgre fritillary butterfly, whooping crane, wolverine, wood frog

Grizzly bear

Endangered Plants: clay-loving wild buckwheat, Dudley Bluffs bladderpod, Dudley Bluffs twinpod, Manco's milk vetch, North Park phacelia, Osterhout milk vetch, Penland beardtongue, spineless hedgehog cactus, Uinta Basin hookless cactus

WHERE THE COLUMBINES GROW

The white and lavender Rocky Mountain columbine was declared the state flower on April 4, 1899. In 1915, after a camping trip, Professor Arthur J. Flynn of Denver wrote this tribute to the beautiful flower. The graceful waltz was adopted as the state song that same year.

TIMELINE

Colorado History

c. AD 1 The Basket Makers settle in the Mesa Verde region.

c. 750 The people at Mesa Verde begin building pueblos, large, apartment-like dwellings, in the sides of cliffs.

c. 1300 The people of Mesa Verde abandon their cliff dwellings.

1598 The Spanish explorer Juan de Oñate reaches the area of present-day Colorado.

1765 Juan Maria de Rivera explores the area around the San Juan Mountains and the Gunnison River.

1803 The United States obtains much of northeastern Colorado through the Louisiana Purchase.

1806 Army officer Zebulon Pike explores Colorado and sees the mountain that will eventually bear his name.

1848 The United States receives western Colorado from Mexico after America's victory in the Mexican-American War.

1851 The first permanent non–Native American settlement in Colorado is established at San Luis.

1858 Gold is discovered near Denver; thousands of miners rush to Colorado in the Pikes Peak gold rush.

1860 Auraria and Denver City merge with a third village to form Denver.

1861 The Colorado Territory is formed.

1867 Denver is named the territorial capital.

1869 The last battle in Colorado between U.S. soldiers and Native Americans is fought at Summit Springs on the plains.

1870 The Denver Pacific and Kansas Pacific railroads connect Colorado to the eastern United States.

1876 Colorado, the Centennial State, becomes the thirty-eighth state.

1877 A silver strike at Leadville sets off a silver boom for Colorado.

1891 Gold is discovered at Cripple Creek.

1894 Women can vote in Colorado state elections for the first time.

1906 The United States Mint in Denver begins producing coins.

1929 The bridge across the Royal Gorge, the world's highest suspension bridge, opens.

1942 Ten thousand Japanese Americans from the West Coast are taken to an internment camp near Grenada, Colorado, because of fears they might aid Japan during World War II.

1957 The Colorado-Big Thompson Project for supplying water to Colorado farmland is completed.

1958 The United States Air Force Academy opens near Colorado Springs.

1983 Federico Peña becomes the first Hispanic mayor of Denver.

1995 Denver's $5.3 billion, state-of-the-art international airport opens.

1999 Columbine High School shootings take place.

ECONOMY

Agricultural Products: apples, barley, beans, cattle, cherries, chickens, corn, dairy products, eggs, hay, hogs, onions, peaches, potatoes, sheep and lambs, sorghum, sugar beets, wheat

Manufactured Products: computers, electrical equipment, fabricated metal products, medical instruments, mining machinery, office equipment, printed materials, scientific instruments, soft drinks, beer

Natural Resources: coal, copper, gold, granite, lead, limestone, molybdenum, natural gas, petroleum, sand and gravel, silver, tungsten, uranium, plutonium, vanadium, zinc

Business and Trade: communications, data processing, engineering, finance, insurance, real estate, tourism, transportation, wholesale and retail sales

Wheat field

CALENDAR OF CELEBRATIONS

National Western Stock Show and Rodeo Every January Denver hosts the world's biggest livestock show. The celebration starts with a parade and is followed by a rodeo, livestock auctions, and a petting arena for children.

Winter Carnival The longest-running winter fair west of the Mississippi River is held in Steamboat Springs every February. The festive carnival includes a week of downhill and cross-country ski races, ski jumping, and other winter fun.

Denver Powwow Native Americans from almost seventy tribes gather for this annual March event. Visitors can watch Native American dancers, drummers, and artists celebrate their traditional ways.

Crane Festival This March festival celebrates the return of whooping and sandhill cranes to the San Luis Valley. There are bus tours, art exhibits, and lectures on wildlife during this popular Monte Vista festival.

Mountain Man Rendezvous Visitors to this annual April event can view a reenactment of Colorado's mountain-man days, with period costumes, ax-throwing and black powder shooting contests, and old-time cooking and crafts. This colorful festival is held in Kit Carson.

Territory Days Every May Colorado's pre-state history is celebrated in Colorado Springs. Events include games, contests, and a make-believe gunfight.

National Western Stock Show and Rodeo

Cinco de Mayo This beloved Mexican holiday honoring a decisive Mexican military victory over French forces in 1862 is celebrated in Denver every May 5. The festival features ethnic foods, music, and dancing.

Aspen Music Festival Famous artists from around the world come to Aspen to perform classical and chamber music as well as opera at this nine-week event. Take a picnic lunch and sit on the lawn at your choice of several concert sites to hear some beautiful music.

Strawberry Days This annual Glenwood Springs fair features a carnival, arts and crafts, and lots of strawberries. The celebration is held every June.

Bluegrass Festival Bluegrass and country music are the main attractions at this June festival. You can listen to all the beautiful sounds while enjoying the great outdoors in Telluride, a popular skiing site in winter.

Aerial Weekend Look to the skies at this July festival in Crested Butte. There are hot-air balloons, hang gliding, and many fun activities for kids.

Dinosaur Days Visitors can watch a dinosaur parade, participate in a fossil dig, and listen to band concerts. Dinosaur Days are held in July in Grand Junction.

Pikes Peak Highland Games and Celtic Festival The region's Scottish heritage is celebrated during this July festival held in Colorado Springs. Traditional Scottish games are played, and there is music, dancing, and food.

Cinco de Mayo celebration

Folklife Festival This July festival in Buena Vista celebrates the folk traditions and arts and crafts of Colorado's European, Native American, and Hispanic ancestors.

Boom Days Leadville hosts this August festival in memory of the gold and silver booms of long ago. Mine-drilling competitions and a pack burro race are highlights of the festival, but there is also a carnival, music, and food.

Colorado State Fair All of the best of Colorado can be enjoyed at the state fair. There are livestock shows and auctions, rides, food, and big-name entertainment. The fair starts in August in Pueblo.

Vail Fest Street entertainment, a yodeling contest, and footraces are just a part of this Vail celebration. The September festival also has sing-alongs, games, and dancing.

Apple Fest This annual October event at Cedaredge celebrates the region's apple harvest. The festival includes arts and crafts, square dancing, and food.

Western Arts, Film, and Cowboy Poetry Gathering Real cowboys gather in Durango in October to share their poetry. The celebration also features demonstrations of cowboy skills, art, and film.

Catch the Glow Estes Park celebrates the holiday season with this November event, which includes holiday lights, clowns, puppeteers, carolers, and an evening parade.

Christmas 1846 at Bent's Old Fort See what Christmas was like on the old frontier. This reenactment brings holidays past to life in this December La Junta celebration.

STATE STARS

Katharine Lee Bates (1859–1929) was a Wellesley College professor from Massachusetts. The view from the top of Pikes Peak inspired her to write the words to "America the Beautiful" in 1893.

Jim Beckwourth (1798–1866), an African-American mountain man, ran trading posts in the Rocky Mountains. He is also believed to have helped found the town of Pueblo.

William Bent (1809–1869) was a prominent trader in Colorado in the early part of the nineteenth century. With his brother George, Bent built Bent's Fort in 1833–1834.

Albert Bierstadt (1830–1902) painted beautiful scenes of Colorado, such as *Storm in the Rocky Mountains.* His works helped bring attention to Colorado's stunning natural setting.

Albert Bierstadt

Black Kettle (?–1868) was a Cheyenne leader whose village was destroyed in the 1864 Sand Creek Massacre, even though he had agreed to peace with the U.S. government. Black Kettle was later killed by U.S. troops when his village, in what is today Oklahoma, was raided.

Clara Brown (1803–1885), a former slave, moved to Colorado during the 1859 gold rush. Her home in Central City became a boardinghouse for poor miners as well as a hospital and church.

Margaret Tobin (Molly) Brown (1867–1932), originally of Missouri, became wealthy in the Colorado gold industry. Brown survived the wreck of the "unsinkable" *Titanic*, helping a lifeboat full of passengers to stay alive, earning her nickname the "Unsinkable Molly Brown."

Ben Nighthorse Campbell (1933–   ) was a U.S. senator from Colorado. Campbell, a Native American, is known for dressing in Cheyenne costume on special occasions and for his support of Native-American issues.

Scott Carpenter (1925–   ) was born in Boulder. One of the United States' early astronauts, Carpenter was the second American to orbit Earth during the Mercury 7 mission.

Kit Carson (1809–1868) earned fame as a trapper and scout in Colorado and the West. In 1860 he commanded Fort Garland and was a rancher.

Lon Chaney (1883–1930) was an early big-screen actor best known for his roles in such films as *The Hunchback of Notre Dame* and *The Phantom of the Opera.* Born in Colorado Springs, Chaney was known as the "man of a thousand faces."

Mary Chase (1907–1981) won the 1945 Pulitzer Prize in drama for her play *Harvey,* about a man whose best friend is an imaginary, 6-foot-tall rabbit. Chase was born in Denver.

Ben Nighthorse Campbell

Chipeta (1843–1924) was the wife of the Ute leader Ouray. Like her husband, Chipeta worked to maintain the peace between Native Americans and white settlers in Colorado.

Adolph Coors (1847–1929) came to Colorado from his native Germany. In Golden he founded the Adolph Coors Company in 1880. The company has since grown to become one of the country's largest beer makers.

Jack Dempsey (1895–1983) was the world heavyweight boxing champion from 1919 to 1926. Born in Manassa, he became known as the "Manassa Mauler."

John Denver (1943–1997) was a singer/songwriter originally from Texas. Born Henry John Deutschendorf, he changed his name because of his love for the city. His songs include "Rocky Mountain High" and "I Guess I'd Rather Be in Colorado." Denver also acted, and his film credits include *Oh, God.* He lived in Aspen.

Ralph Edwards (1913–   ), from Merino, has produced a number of well-known television shows. Some of the shows Edwards has worked on include *Truth or Consequences*, *This Is Your Life*, *Name that Tune*, and *The People's Court*.

John Elway (1960–   ) was an outstanding quarterback for the Denver Broncos. His exciting style of playing led the Broncos to five Super Bowls: 1987, 1988, 1990, 1998, and 1999.

John Elway

John Evans (1814–1897) was the territorial governor of Colorado from 1862 to 1865. He founded the school that was to become the University of Denver, and in 1870 he built the Denver Pacific Railroad, linking Colorado to the rest of the country.

Douglas Fairbanks (1883–1939), born in Denver, starred in many action movies in the early years of film. His credits include *The Three Musketeers* and *Robin Hood.* He also helped found the United Artists film company.

Barney Ford (1824–1902) was a fugitive from slavery who joined the Colorado gold rush in 1860. He became the owner of a well-known Denver hotel and helped other fugitive slaves. Ford also started the first classes for African-American adults in Colorado.

Justina Ford (1871–1952) was the first African-American woman to become a medical doctor in Colorado. Ford delivered thousands of babies, mostly for poor black women, in Denver.

Willard Libby (1908–1980) of Grand Valley achieved fame as a chemist by discovering a way to determine the age of ancient materials using radiocarbon testing. He won the 1960 Nobel Prize in Chemistry.

Glenn Miller (1904–1944) grew up in Fort Morgan and attended the University of Colorado. Miller gained fame as a trombone player and leader of the Glenn Miller Band. He died on his way to entertain American troops in World War II when the plane in which he was flying was lost.

Ouray (1833–1880) was a Ute leader who attempted to keep the peace between Native Americans and white settlers. His efforts helped to maintain good relations between the two groups for many years.

David Packard (1912–1996) grew up in Pueblo. In 1939 Packard started the Hewlett-Packard Company along with William Hewlett. The company became an electronics giant and today makes computers and related items.

Federico Peña (1947–   ), a Mexican American, served two terms as mayor of Denver, from 1983 to 1991. Peña was later picked by President Bill Clinton to lead the U.S. Department of Transportation.

Antoinette Perry (1888–1946), born in Denver, was a popular stage actress in the early 1900s. The Tony Award, which is given each year to the best actors in theater, is named for Perry, whose nickname was Tony.

Zebulon Pike (1779–1813) was a famous explorer of the American West. Pike first spotted the mountain that was to be named after him in 1806.

Denver Pyle (1920–1997), from Bethune, was a well-known face in movies and on television. Pyle had roles in *Bonnie and Clyde*, *The Life and Times of Grizzly Adams*, and *The Dukes of Hazzard*.

Florence Sabin (1871–1953) became well known for her work combating the disease tuberculosis. Born in Central City, she was the first woman chosen to join the National Academy of Sciences.

Patricia Schroeder (1940–   ) was Colorado's first woman to serve in the U.S. Congress. Schroeder was elected to the House of Representatives in 1973 and served until 1996.

Patricia Schroeder

Byron White (1917–2002) was born in Fort Collins. A college and pro football star, White studied law and was named to the U.S. Supreme Court by President John F. Kennedy in 1962.

TOUR THE STATE

Dinosaur National Monument (Dinosaur) While the dinosaur bones are found on the Utah side of this national site, the Colorado side offers beautiful views and hiking trails.

Hot Springs Pool (Glenwood Springs) Heated by mineral hot springs to a temperature of 90 degrees Fahrenheit, the pool here, over two blocks long, is open year-round. There's also a huge, twisting water slide.

Colorado Ski Heritage Museum (Vail) The history of skiing in Colorado is presented through pictures and such artifacts as old skis and chairlifts. There is also a video on the history of Vail.

Lomax Placer Gulch Tour (Breckenridge) Tour a miner's cabin and find out how Colorado's old-time miners searched for gold at this fun site. You can even swirl a miner's pan in water to find some flecks of real gold.

Rocky Mountain National Park (Estes Park) This beautiful national park offers everything from fishing to hiking to rock climbing. There are some 355 miles of hiking trails, many of which are suitable for children.

Georgetown Viewing Station (Georgetown) Through the viewing scopes at this station you can often spot Rocky Mountain bighorn sheep during the winter. You may even be able to hear the crack of male sheep's horns as they fight for leadership of the herd.

St. Mary's Glacier (Idaho Springs) Not only can you view a glacier here, but you can actually walk on it. Scenic hiking paths circle around St. Mary's Lake and lead up to the glacier.

Buffalo Bill Memorial Museum and Grave (Golden) One of the West's greatest legendary figures, Buffalo Bill Cody, is remembered in this museum. Learn about his life through the dioramas, artifacts, clothes, photos, and paintings on display.

Black American West Museum and Heritage Center (Denver) Learn about the history of African Americans in the American West, especially African-American cowboys, through the artifacts and pictures in this museum, which is located in a historic home.

Children's Museum (Denver) Reporting the weather on the museum's TV station, exploring a beehive, and touching a live snake are just a few of the things you can do here. Outside the museum is KidSlope, an artificial ski slope where young visitors can learn to ski year-round.

Denver Museum of Natural History (Denver) Visitors young and old can learn about everything from dinosaurs to gold nuggets to the stars at this exciting museum. At the Hall of Life, museumgoers can test and find out about their own fitness.

United States Mint (Denver) On a tour of the Denver mint you can see how the coins jingling in your pocket are made. Visitors can see the new coins pouring out of stamping machines and being counted and bagged.

Plains Conservation Center (Aurora) Animals living inside the center include badgers, prairie dogs, coyotes, jackrabbits, owls, and eagles. Special guided tours offer you the chance to see the wildlife and plants of the prairie and to hear educational lectures.

Centennial Village (Greeley) The buildings at this site reflect life in Colorado from 1860 to 1920. There are homes of all sorts, ranging from a mansion to a poor homestead shack, a schoolhouse, a tepee, a blacksmith shop, and much more.

Cave of the Winds (Manitou Springs) Narrow passages and winding paths, colorfully lit, lead you through twenty underground "rooms" full of impressive stalagmites and stalactites. There is also an outdoor laser light show held in the evenings.

Cave of the Winds

Garden of the Gods (Colorado Springs) Incredible red sandstone formations are the attractions at this impressive site. Stone formations with names like Balanced Rock and Kissing Camels glow brightly in both the rising and setting sun.

United States Air Force Academy (Colorado Springs) Visitors to the Academy can see a short film about the school and watch as cadets march to the dining hall and practice parachute jumps. The Cadet Chapel is one of Colorado's most recognized buildings.

Pikes Peak and Pike National Forest (Colorado Springs) Beautiful views are the prime attraction of a climb up Pikes Peak. Denver, seventy-five miles away, can often be seen from the top. The summit can be reached by trail, road, or cog railway, a train specially fitted for steep inclines.

El Pueblo Museum (Pueblo) The exhibits explore the heritage of the Pueblo area. There are saddles on which to climb, a full-size tepee to explore, displays on children's clothing from the nineteenth century, and more.

Bent's Old Fort National Historic Site (La Junta) The fort here is a reconstruction of Bent's Fort as it looked in 1845. Visitors can explore such areas as the kitchen, blacksmith and carpenter shops, and rooms that would have been the quarters of trappers and soldiers.

Royal Gorge Bridge (Cañon City) The Royal Gorge Bridge is the highest suspension bridge in the world, and a walk across it can be exciting and scary. There is also an aerial tram that goes over the gorge, an incline railway that climbs up the side of the gorge, and a train that runs through the bottom of the gorge.

Great Sand Dunes National Monument (Alamosa) The dunes at this site can reach seven hundred feet high, the tallest in North America. Hiking over the dunes is permitted, though it can be tiring work.

Mesa Verde National Park (Durango) Exploring this amazing site, the home of the region's Anasazi people seven hundred years ago, often requires climbing 10-foot ladders and crawling through tunnels. A museum here helps explain the Anasazi culture and the cliffside homes.

Black Canyon of the Gunnison National Park (Montrose) The 2,500-foot-high walls of this canyon make for breathtaking views. In some places the walls seem to have been painted by an artist. The area has many short hiking trails.

Fort Uncompahgre Living History Museum (Delta) Dressed as the inhabitants of the fort would have been in 1826, guides help bring this site alive. They carry out everyday activities at this re-created fur-trading post and allow visitors to join in.

Dinosaur Valley Museum (Grand Junction) This attraction has giant robotic dinosaurs as well as real dinosaur skeletons and footprints. You can even watch workers in the lab as they carefully chip away at rock to reveal fossils.

Dinosaur Valley Museum

FUN FACTS

The only city in the United States that gets its water from the melting ice of a glacier is Boulder. Boulder's water supply comes from the Arapahoe Glacier, northwest of the city.

In 1929 Bill Williams rolled a peanut to the top of Pikes Peak using his nose. The task took him twenty days.

A 1990 hailstorm, the most costly in U.S. history, caused $650 million worth of damage in Colorado.

The Barbie doll was invented by a Denver woman named Ruth Handler in 1959.

Find Out More

To find out more about the Mile-High State, check your school or local library or a good bookstore for these items.

BOOKS

Bograd, Larry. *Uniquely Colorado.* Chicago: Heinemann Library, 2003.

Miller, Amy. *Colorado* (From Sea to Shining Sea series). Danbury, CT: Children's Press, 2002.

Speaker-Yuan, Margaret. *The Royal Gorge Bridge* (Building World Landmarks series). San Diego: Blackbirch Press, 2003.

VIDEOS

Bennett-Watt Media. *Discover America: Colorado.* 2003.

———. *Discover Pikes Peak Country Colorado.* Finley Holiday Film Corporation, no date.

Michener, James A. *Centennial.* Universal City, CA: MCA Universal Home Video, 1995.

WEB SITES

In addition to the sites below, you can always use a search engine to search, for example, a famous name, a park or monument, or the name of a city.

Official Site of the State of Colorado

www.colorado.gov

This is Colorado's frequently updated home page, with information about living there or visiting.

Colorado Historical Society

www.coloradohistory.org

This is the home page of the Colorado Historical Society, which has many interesting listings.

Colorado Division of Wildlife

www.wildlife.state.co.us

The Colorado Division of Wildlife's page includes information on hunting and fishing in the state, animal habitats, education, news and information, and an interactive kid's page.

Index

Page numbers in **boldface** are illustrations and charts.